A $$8.65

A CONCISE
INTRODUCTION TO LOGIC

Second Edition

A CONCISE INTRODUCTION TO LOGIC

Second Edition

Robert W. Burch
Texas A&M University

Wadsworth Publishing Company
Belmont, California
A Division of Wadsworth, Inc.

Philosophy Editor: Kenneth King

Copy Editor: Jackie Estrada

ISBN   0-534-03868-9

Printed in the United States of America

1 2 3 4 5 6 7 8 9 10---88 87 86 85

PREFACE

This study guide is intended to be used in conjunction with Patrick
J. Hurley's *A Concise Introduction to Logic*. In it you will find summary
statements of the main points made in the Hurley text. You will also
find illustrations of these points, worked examples, and original problems for practice. Each section is closely coordinated with a corresponding section of Hurley's text. You should read a given section of the text
thoroughly, then try to work some of the exercises in the text. Then refer to the corresponding section of the study guide. Follow through the
worked exercises and examples, and attempt to work out the exercises in
the study guide. You may check your comprehension by comparing your solu-
tions with those given at the back of the study guide: answers to all
original exercises are provided.

Introductory logic is a subject best learned by practice. It is a
skill as much as a body of knowledge, and like other skills it must be
regularly exercised in order to be acquired and retained. Try to think
of logic as you would tennis or bowling: you may know very well in the
abstract what is to be done, and you may understand very well when others
do it, but you may still not be able to do it yourself. Doing it yourself is really the only way to acquire the ability to do logic. So try
to practice regularly; work as many exercises as you can on your own.
You will find your ability and your confidence increasing. And don't be
surprised if it is even fun.

CONTENTS

1
BASIC CONCEPTS

1.1 ARGUMENTS, PREMISES, AND CONCLUSIONS

Logic is the science that evaluates arguments. An *argument* is a group of statements, one of which (the *conclusion*) is claimed, implicitly or explicitly, to follow from the others (the *premises*). The premises of an argument set forth the evidence for the conclusion; the conclusion is claimed to follow from this evidence. The primary task of logic is to distinguish between good arguments (those in which the conclusion really does follow from the premises) and bad arguments (those in which the conclusion does not in fact follow from the premises, even though it is claimed to do so).

In analyzing arguments, it is crucial to distinguish premises from conclusion. Sometimes premises precede the conclusion, but sometimes they do not. In order to distinguish premises from conclusion, one must understand the relation that the statements in an argument have to each other. This relation is often signaled by certain *indicator words*, such as "therefore," "hence," and "so," which indicate conclusions, and "because," "since," and "for," which indicate premises.

A first step in analyzing an argument is to restructure it, putting the premises first and the conclusion last. Thus, the argument "Socrates must be mortal, since he is a man and all men are mortal," may be restructured as:

> Socrates is a man. ⎫
> All men are mortal. ⎭   *premises*
>
> Therefore, Socrates is mortal.   *conclusion*

Notice that the clause "he is a man" in the original argument has been replaced by the sentence "Socrates is a man" in the restructured argument. This reflects the fact that in arguments *statements* are used to express *propositions*, the meaning-contents of statements. Thus, when the word "he" is used to refer to Socrates, the statements "he is a man" and "Socrates is a man" express the same proposition; that is, they have the same meaning-content. If we want to be subtle, we can say that arguments consist of propositions but they are expressed by statements. In practice, however, we can typically ignore the distinction between propositions and statements, provided that we are careful to understand and accurately reexpress the meanings of the statements in the argument.

Notice also that the word "must" in "Socrates must be mortal" is used as an indicator of the status of the statement "Socrates is mortal" as a conclusion. The premises are not meant to show that "Socrates *has*

1

to be mortal," in the sense that it is impossible that he be otherwise; what *has to be* is that he *is* mortal *if* he is a man and all men are mortal. The word "since" in the original argument is used as an indicator of both of the premises.

Sample Exercises from Exercise 1.1, Part I

1. Catherine most likely will not be going to the concert tonight because her car has a dead battery and she has no other means of transportation.

    Restructured form:

    P₁: Catherine's car has a dead battery.
    P₂: Catherine has no other means of transportation.
    C: Catherine most likely will not be going to the concert tonight.

    In this example, the key fact is that the premises are indicated by the word "because."

2. This wine tastes sweet, so it can't be Cabernet.

    Restructured form:

    P: This wine tastes sweet.
    C: This wine is not Cabernet.

    The word "so" indicates the conclusion. Also, the modal word "can't" helps to indicate the conclusion. Notice that there is only one premise in this example.

3. The California condor is threatened with extinction inasmuch as the condor population has been decreasing yearly and fewer than fifty birds are alive at this time.

    Restructured form:

    P₁: The California condor population has been decreasing yearly.
    P₂: Fewer than fifty California condors are alive at this time.
    C: The California condor is threatened with extinction.

    The indicator words "inasmuch as" signal that the following two statements are premises of this argument.

4. Chicago is either in Illinois or Wisconsin. But it's not in Wisconsin. It follows that Chicago is in Illinois.

    Restructured form:

    P₁: Chicago is either in Illinois or Wisconsin.
    P₂: Chicago is not in Wisconsin.
    C: Chicago is in Illinois.

    The conclusion of this argument is indicated by the phrase "It follows that."

Additional Exercises for Section 1.1

Put the following arguments into a restructured form, indicating premises and conclusion and placing premises first.

1. Only a fool or a daredevil smokes cigarettes, since cigarette smoking is a leading cause of cancer.

2. If we had world enough and time, this coyness would not be a crime. But we don't have world enough and time. So this coyness is a crime.

3. The square root of the number two is an irrational number. It follows that the hypotenuse of an isosceles right triangle is not commensurable with its side.

4. No man is an island. Every man is a piece of the continent, a part of the main. Therefore, no one should send to know for whom the bell tolls.

5. A free market is necessary for a free society. For without the freedom to buy and sell, the freedom to speak is absent. Moreover, in the absence of a free market, tyranny flourishes.

6. He jests at scars that never felt a wound. So Mercutio must never have felt a wound, since he jests at scars.

7. The French are the most intelligent people in the world. For it takes years and years for adult Americans to learn to speak the French language well. But in France even little children speak it well.

8. The world must have existed from eternity. For if not, then at some time there was nothing at all. And out of nothing at all nothing at all could come.

9. The world must have existed from eternity. Therefore, since eternity includes 6006 B.C., the world must have existed in 6006 B.C.

10. There are many average families in the United States. It follows that many U.S. families have parts of children in them, because the average U.S. family has 2.2 children and two-tenths of a child is a part of a child.

1.2 RECOGNIZING ARGUMENTS

It is important to distinguish arguments from nonargumentative passages. In an argument, at least one of the statements must present evidence, and there must be a claim, implicit or explicit, that something follows from the evidence. Words that are indicators of premises and conclusions are useful clues to, but not guarantees of, the presence of an argument. Typical indicator words can function to signal passages of sorts other than arguments, and arguments may contain no indicator words. "I don't like ice cream because the cold hurts my teeth" contains the indicator word "because," but it is an explanation, not an argument. "Aerial spraying of the Mediterranean fruit fly should be allowed; the fruit fly

3

spreads rapidly, is extremely prolific, and is little affected by ground
spraying" is an argument, even though it contains no indicator words.

Typical kinds of nonarguments are *descriptive reports, exhortations,
warnings, pieces of advice, aphorisms, statements of belief, statements
of opinion, illustrations, conditional statements,* and *explanations.*

Illustrations, conditional statements, and explanations are the
types of nonarguments most apt to be confused with arguments. Illustrations can be confused with arguments because they often contain the word
"thus," one of the typical indicator words. Here is an example: "Many
painters have taken as their real subject some abstract theme. Thus,
Goya and Picasso, each in his own way—Goya's *The Disasters of War* series
and Picasso's painting *Guernica*—explore the pain and horror of warfare."
The idea of this passage is to illustrate a general point, not to prove
it.

A conditional statement is an "if . . . then" statement, such as "If
the air pressure lowers, then the barometer falls." The statement immediately following the "if" (here "the air pressure lowers") is called the
antecedent of the conditional; the statement following the "then" (here
"the barometer falls") is called the *consequent.* Occasionally, the word
"then" in a conditional statement may be omitted. Conditional statements
look like arguments; that is, a conditional statement looks like an argument in which the antecedent is the premise and the consequent is the
conclusion. But in a conditional statement no commitment is being made,
even imaginatively, to the truth either of the antecedent or of the consequent. What the conditional asserts is merely that *if* the antecedent
is true, the consequent is true. In an argument, however, some sort of
commitment—even if only for the sake of arguing—is made to the truth
of the premises.

One reason conditional statements look like arguments is that they
express a transition in thought from one statement, the antecedent, to
another, the consequent. An argument also expresses such a transition
from its premises to its conclusion. In fact, the transition expressed
in a conditional sentence may be reexpressed in the form of an argument
that has the antecedent of the conditional as its premise and the consequent as its conclusion. For instance, the transition in the conditional "If the air pressure lowers, then the barometer falls" can be
reexpressed in the form of an argument: "The air pressure lowers.
Therefore, the barometer falls."

Even though conditional statements are not by themselves arguments,
they may serve as premises or conclusions of arguments. Here is an
argument containing a conditional statement as a premise:

If the air pressure lowers, then the barometer falls.
The air pressure just lowered.
Therefore, the barometer just fell.

Here is an argument containing a conditional statement as conclusion:

The higher the altitude, the lower the air pressure.
At higher altitudes the barometer falls.
We may conclude that if the air pressure lowers, then the
barometer falls.

Explanations may be confused with arguments because they typically
contain such indicator words as "because" or "for the reason that."
Also explanations, like arguments, consist of two components: the
explanandum (the state or event that is explained—or, more precisely,

the description of this state or event) and the *explanans* (the statements that do the explaining). Thus, in "I don't like ice cream because the cold hurts my teeth," the explanandum is "I don't like ice cream" and the explanans is "the cold hurts my teeth." Explanations are not arguments because they do not claim to prove or justify that something is the case. In "I don't like ice cream because the cold hurts my teeth," it is not being claimed that my not liking ice cream is proven or demonstrated. My not liking ice cream is taken for granted; what the explanation does is to account for *why* I don't like ice cream.

Sample Exercises from Exercise 1.2, Part I

1. The price of gold increased yesterday because of increased tensions in the Middle East.

   As typically spoken or written, this passage would not be an argument. It would be already known and taken for granted *that* the price of gold increased yesterday, so the point of the passage would not be to establish this fact. Rather, the passage attempts to explain *why* the price of gold increased.

2. If public education fails to improve the quality of instruction in both primary and secondary schools, then it is likely that it will lose additional students to the private sector in the years ahead.

   Here no commitment is made to the truth of the statement that public education will fail to improve the quality of instruction in both primary and secondary schools. The passage simply states that *if* this happens *then* it is likely that public education will lose additional students to the private sector in the years ahead. The passage is not an argument but rather a conditional statement.

3. Freedom of the press is the most important of our constitutionally guaranteed freedoms. Without it, our other freedoms would be immediately threatened. Furthermore, it provides the fulcrum for the advancement of new freedoms.

   This passage clearly claims to prove something, namely that freedom of the press is the most important of our constitutionally guaranteed freedoms. The first statement of the passage is thus the conclusion of the argument the passage constitutes, and the remaining two statements present the premises for this conclusion.

4. The Swiss Alps contain a number of very high peaks. Thus, the Weisshorn, Matterhorn, and Nadelhorn are all over 14,000 feet.

   This passage does not attempt to prove anything. Rather, its second sentence exemplifies the general statement made by its first sentence.

Additional Exercises for Section 1.2

Determine whether the following passages constitute arguments. For each argument, identify its conclusion.

1. The reason the beaker exploded is that it contained nitroglycerin and was shaken violently.

5

2. The reason it is undoubtable that there are flying saucers is that many people have seen them with their own eyes.

3. John did not feel very lively, so he probably ate something that did not agree with him.

4. John did not feel very lively, so he stayed home from the dance.

5. If you want a cup of coffee, you may have one.

6. If you want a cup of coffee, you are addicted to caffeine.

7. Several nations now possess the technology to manufacture nuclear weapons, even though they may not actually have built such weapons. Thus, South Africa has a number of atomic power plants and many laboratories in which fissionable material may be isolated.

8. Several nations now possess the technology to manufacture nuclear weapons, even though they may not actually have built such weapons. Thus, the world is in much greater danger of a nuclear confrontation than one might at first think.

9. Prices escalate almost daily. This inflationary tendency in our economy is one of its most disturbing features. No one wants to have to pay more for an item tomorrow than he pays for it today.

10. Prices escalate almost daily. This inflationary tendency in our economy is one of its most disturbing features. A government cannot be considered responsible if it does not deal with this problem.

1.3 DEDUCTION AND INDUCTION

Two different standards may be used to evaluate arguments: the deductive standard and the inductive standard. The convention is that the argument itself is deductive if the deductive standard is more appropriately applied to it, and inductive if the inductive standard is more appropriately applied to it. According to the deductive standard, an argument is considered good only if its conclusion follows *necessarily* from its premises; while according to the inductive standard, an argument is good only if its conclusion follows *probably* from its premises.

In deciding whether an argument is deductive or inductive, that is to say whether it is best to apply to the argument the deductive or the inductive standard, several factors must be borne in mind. First, there is the nature of the link between premises and conclusion. If the conclusion follows, or is thought to follow necessarily from the premises, the deductive standard is more relevant and the argument is regarded as deductive. Otherwise it is usually better to regard the argument as inductive. Second, special indicator words should be taken into account. In drawing its conclusion, if the argument employs such words as "necessarily," "certainly," or "absolutely," it is usually regarded as deductive. If words such as "probably," "likely," or "plausibly" are employed, the argument is usually regarded as inductive. Third, the form of the argument helps determine whether it is deductive or inductive. For example, arguments that depend on some mathematical principle, arguments from definition, or arguments framed as syllogisms (to be studied later),

6

are best treated as deductive. There are several common types of inductive arguments, including *predictions about the future, arguments from analogy, inductive generalizations, arguments based on signs,* and *causal inferences.*

In a *prediction about the future*, the premises refer to matters in the present or past, and the conclusion is about some matter in the future. An *argument from analogy* depends on the existence of a similarity between two things or states of affairs. For example, someone might conclude that ostriches can fly because they have wings, and other creatures with wings are known to fly. An *inductive generalization* argues from knowledge about a sample of a group of things to a claim about the entire group. An *argument based on signs* proceeds from the knowledge of a certain sign to a knowledge of the thing or situation that sign signifies. For example, from a sign saying "Danger" one might conclude that the area in which the sign is located contains something dangerous. *Causal inferences* argue from knowledge of causes to claims about effects, or conversely from knowledge of effects to claims about causes. If I conclude, from knowledge that a tornado hit a certain town, that the damage in the town was extensive, I argue from cause to effect. If I argue from the presence of ashes on the carpet to the claim that someone was smoking in the room, I argue from effect to cause.

Sample Exercises from Exercise 1.3, Part I

1. Because triangle A is congruent with triangle B, and triangle A is isosceles, it follows that triangle B is isosceles.

    This argument, like most arguments in mathematics, is deductive. The point of the argument is to prove absolutely that triangle B is isosceles, for it states that triangle A is isosceles and that triangle B coincides with it in every respect—that is, that B may be placed in A's position and they would coincide point for point (that is the meaning of the word "congruent"). Even though the likeness between A and B is appealed to in this argument, it is still *not* an argument from analogy, for the gist of the argument makes it clear that the conclusion is meant to follow necessarily from the premises.

2. The sign on the candy machine reads "Out of Order." The candy machine must be broken.

    This argument proceeds from a sign to what the sign signifies and is thus an inductive argument based on signs. It is not deductive because someone who argues this way is surely not thinking that the machine absolutely has to be broken: surely he knows that there are various ways it could happen that the sign could be there and the machine still not be broken. The argument is not a causal inference either—the brokenness of the machine is not the cause of the sign's being in place, and (even more obviously) the sign's being in place is not the cause of the machine's brokenness.

3. The annual rainfall in Seattle has been over 15 inches every year for the past 30 years. Therefore, the annual rainfall next year will probably be over 15 inches.

    This argument is inductive, as the word "probably" indicates. It is a prediction about the future.

7

4. All guitar players are musicians, and some guitar players are not astronauts. It follows that some musicians are not astronauts.

   This deductive argument is recognizable by its format: It is a categorical syllogism (see text).

Additional Exercises for Section 1.3

Determine whether the following arguments are deductive or inductive; if an argument is inductive, identify its type.

   1. Texans must all wear cowboy boots; I went to Houston last Thursday and everyone I saw on the street had boots on.

   2. Even numbers yield even numbers when they are squared. It follows that the square roots of odd perfect squares are odd.

   3. We can go out of the theater at the front; the Exit sign points in that direction.

   4. Look at these footprints in the mud by the window. We must have a peeping Tom.

   5. This fish looks very similar to a trout or a salmon. Since those fish are tasty, this one must be tasty, too.

   6. Of course the sun will rise tomorrow—it's risen every day in human history.

   7. Everyone who is well educated knows about the existence of the Roman Empire, and John is well educated. So he has to know something about the Roman Empire.

   8. Everyone who has ever tried to climb the Matterhorn has experienced terror at some stage of the ascent. Just you wait, John; sooner or later on your climb you are going to be afraid.

   9. If you found a model of the solar system, you'd know that someone made it. How much more obvious it is, then, that the real solar system must have been made by somebody.

   10. This circle has an area of exactly 4 square inches. So a circle with an area of 1 square inch would have a radius half as long.

1.4 VALIDITY, TRUTH, SOUNDNESS, STRENGTH, COGENCY

A deductive argument is either *valid* or *invalid*. Validity does not admit of amount or degree: an argument is either valid, period, or invalid, period; there is no middle ground. A deductive argument is valid if the conclusion follows necessarily from the premises—that is, if it is necessarily the case that if the premises were to be true (whether they are in fact true or not), the conclusion would have to be true (whether it is in fact true or not). Otherwise, a deductive argument is invalid. If there is any possibility that the premises could all be true and yet the conclusion false, then the argument is invalid.

Notice that true premises and a true conclusion are not required for validity. Indeed, there can be valid arguments with false premises and a false conclusion—for example, "Dogs have five legs; therefore, dogs have an odd number of legs." The only possibility ruled out by the validity of an argument is that it have all true premises and a false conclusion. Also notice that true premises and a true conclusion do not by any means assure validity. There are invalid arguments with true premises and a true conclusion—for example, "Dogs have four legs; therefore, birds have two legs."

A *sound argument* is a deductive argument that is valid and has all true premises. Obviously, in a sound argument the conclusion will be true, too.

An inductive argument is either *strong* or *weak*. Unlike validity, the strength of an inductive argument *does* admit of amount or degree; an inductive argument A and an inductive argument B may both be strong and yet A may be stronger than B. For example, suppose A is "Ninety percent of the mice in Australia have been examined and found to be white; therefore, probably all of the mice in Australia are white." This is a strong argument. But if B is "Ninety-nine percent of the mice in Australia have been examined and found to be white; therefore, probably all of the mice in Australia are white," then B is even stronger than A. An inductive argument is strong if on the basis of the assumption that its premises are true, its conclusion probably is true; otherwise, it is weak. An inductive argument having true premises but a probably false conclusion is weak; but aside from this fact strength and weakness have no more direct relation to the truth or falsity of premises and conclusion than do the validity and invalidity of deductive arguments.

A *cogent* argument is an inductive argument that is strong and has all true premises. Obviously, in a strong argument the conclusion will probably be true, too.

Sample Exercises from Exercise 1.4, Part I

1. Since *Moby Dick* was written by Shakespeare, and *Moby Dick* is a science fiction novel, it follows that Shakespeare wrote a science fiction novel.

   Both premises of this argument are false; therefore, the argument is clearly not sound. However, the argument is nevertheless valid, because if it were the case that Shakespeare wrote *Moby Dick* and that *Moby Dick* were a science fiction novel, then it would have to be the case that Shakespeare wrote a science fiction novel.

2. If George Washington was beheaded, then George Washington died. George Washington died. Therefore, George Washington was beheaded.

   We may safely regard both premises of this argument to be true. The conclusion, however, is false. No valid argument can have true premises and a false conclusion, so this argument is invalid. All invalid arguments are unsound, so this one is unsound.

9

Sample Exercises from Exercise 1.4, Part II

1. This die is marked with numbers 1 through 6. Therefore, probably the next roll will turn up a 6.

   In this inductive argument the premise is true (as we know from the instructions to the exercise). The conclusion, however, is probably false, because there is only one way the die can turn up a 6 and there are five ways it can fail to turn up a 6. Therefore, this is a weak inductive argument, and as such it is not cogent.

2. This die is marked with numbers 1 through 6. Therefore, probably the next roll will turn up a number less than 6.

   The premise is true in this argument. The conclusion is probably true because there are five ways the die can turn up a number less than 6 and there is only one way it can fail to turn up a number less than 6. So this is a strong inductive argument. Since it also has a true premise (its only premise), it is a cogent argument.

Additional Exercises for Section 1.4

Determine whether the following arguments are deductive or inductive. If the argument is deductive, determine whether it is valid or invalid. If the argument is inductive, determine whether it is strong or weak.

1. This is a standard deck of playing cards. So probably if I draw a card at random from it, that card will be a king.

2. This is a standard deck of playing cards. So if I draw a card at random from it, fifty-one cards will remain.

3. This is a standard deck of playing cards. So if I draw a card at random from it, that card will probably not be a spade.

4. We know that the murderer was either Jackson or Harrison. We also know the murderer could not have been Harrison. So the murderer had to be Jackson.

5. We know that the murderer was either Jackson or Harrison. So probably the murderer was Jackson.

6. Every number evenly divisible by 4 is evenly divisible by 2. Therefore, no number evenly divisible by 4 is odd.

7. If dogs have more than five legs, then they have more than four legs. Dogs do not have more than five legs. Therefore, dogs do not have more than four legs.

8. John has a favorite color among those in the spectrum. So it is probably red.

9. For quite a while every fourth United States president has died while in office. Ronald Reagan is the fourth president after Kennedy, who died in office. It is likely, then, that Ronald Reagan will die in office.

10. Every sample of copper ever examined conducts electricity. So it is a safe bet that this particular piece of copper will conduct electricity when we examine it.

1.5 PROVING INVALIDITY: THE COUNTEREXAMPLE METHOD

The validity of an argument is to a large extent independent of its subject matter and is, instead, dependent on the *form* or *structure* of the argument. For instance, consider the argument form

> All *A* are *B*.
> All *B* are *C*.
> Therefore, all *A* are *C*.

where *A*, *B*, and *C* stand for terms designating types of things. No matter what these letters stand for, the resulting argument will be a valid one. Thus, this is a *valid argument form*. An *invalid argument form* is one that has at least one substitution instance that is an invalid argument. (A *substitution instance* of an argument form in general is obtained by replacing the letters in an argument form by terms designating types of things or by statements.) Every substitution instance of a valid argument form is valid, while at least one substitution instance of an invalid argument form must be invalid; indeed, an invalid argument form must have at least one substitution instance in which its premises are actually true and its conclusion false.

We may adopt the following alternative definition of invalidity:

> An argument is invalid if and only if its form allows for a substitution instance having true premises and a false conclusion.

This definition is based on two claims: (1) An argument is invalid if and only if its form is invalid; (2) an argument form is invalid if and only if it has at least one substitution instance in which the premises are true and the conclusion false.

It follows from this alternate definition of invalidity that an argument may be proved invalid by first isolating its logical form and then inventing a substitution instance of this form with true premises and a false conclusion. This method is called the *counterexample* method. For example, the argument

> All elms are plants.
> All trees are plants.
> Therefore, all elms are trees.

has the form

> All *A* are *B*.
> All *C* are *B*.
> Therefore, all *A* are *C*.

But this form has the substitution instance:

> All horses are animals.
> All cows are animals.
> Therefore, all horses are cows.

This argument has true premises and a false conclusion, which shows that the original argument was invalid.

Note of caution: The form of an argument may not be what it seems. Indeed, the form of an argument may be quite obscure. Consider the following valid argument:

> This object is red.
> Therefore, this object is not green.

If we assume that the form of this argument is

> This object is A.
> Therefore, this object is not B.

then we can obtain the following substitution instance:

> This object is a stallion.
> Therefore, this object is not a horse.

This is clearly an argument that has, in the right circumstances, a true premise and a false conclusion. This procedure would show, incorrectly, that the original argument was not valid. The point here is that the isolation of the correct form of an argument may be quite laborious and complicated and that it may depend on the meanings of the terms involved in the argument. As one more example of how difficult it may be to identify the form of an argument correctly, consider the following two arguments, noting the fact that the first one is valid and the second one has true premises and a false conclusion:

> If Chris Evert is the wife of Ronald Reagan, then she is married to him.
> Chris Evert is not the wife of Ronald Reagan.
> Therefore, she is not married to him.

> If Chris Evert is the daughter of Ronald Reagan, then she is younger than him.
> Chris Evert is not the daughter of Ronald Reagan.
> Therefore, she is not younger than him.

Sample Exercises from Section 1.5, Part I

1. All candidates running in this election are liberal-minded individuals, for all astute politicians are candidates running in this election and all liberal-minded individuals are astute politicians.

   This argument has the form

   > All A are C.
   > All L are A.
   > Therefore, all C are L.

> All mammals are animals.
> All dogs are mammals.
> Therefore, all animals are dogs.

Since this argument has true premises and a false conclusion, the original argument is invalid.

2. No zoo keepers are constant complainers, so some constant complainers are underpaid workers, since some underpaid workers are not zoo keepers.

   This argument has the form

   > No Z are C.
   > Some U are not Z.
   > Therefore, some C are U.

   Substitution instance:

   > No dogs are cats.
   > Some fish are not dogs.
   > Therefore, some cats are fish.

   Since this argument has true premises and a false conclusion, the original argument is invalid.

3. Some former athletes are not boring individuals because no talkative cabdrivers are boring individuals and some talkative cabdrivers are former athletes.

   This argument has the form

   > No T are B.
   > Some T are F.
   > Therefore, some F are not B.

   Every substitution instance of this form is valid; for, assuming that some T are F, then there are some things that are both T and F; but since these things are T, then by the first premise they are not B; so they must be both F and yet not B.

4. No basket makers are successful businessmen and all successful businessmen are wealthy entrepreneurs. Thus, no basket makers are wealthy entrepreneurs.

   This argument has the form

   > No B are S.
   > All S are W.
   > Therefore, no B are W.

Substitution instance:

> No cats are dogs.
> All dogs are animals.
> Therefore, no cats are animals.

Since this argument has true premises and a false conclusion, the original argument is invalid.

Additional Exercises for Section 1.5

Identify the form of each of the following arguments and use it to determine whether each argument is valid or invalid. If an argument is invalid, construct a substitution instance of its form in which all the premises are true and the conclusion is false.

1. All fish are vertebrates and all vertebrates belong to the animal kingdom, so all fish belong to the animal kingdom.

2. All fish are vertebrates and some bass are fish. Therefore, some bass are vertebrates.

3. All fish are vertebrates and some bass are vertebrates. Therefore, some bass are fish.

4. No grasshoppers are butterflies, but all monarchs are butterflies. So no grasshoppers are monarchs.

5. No grasshoppers are butterflies, but some moths are butterflies. So no moths are grasshoppers.

6. Some logicians are philosophers, and some logicians are mathematicians. It follows that some philosophers are mathematicians.

7. Some existentialist poets are geniuses, for some madmen are existentialist poets and all geniuses are madmen.

8. Some lovers of music are trombone players. It follows that some trombone players are not jazz musicians, since no jazz musicians are lovers of music.

9. All the brave deserve the fair. None that deserve the fair are faint-hearted. We may conclude that none of the brave are faint-hearted.

10. All tasks are challenges to the industrious. All tasks are burdens to the lazy. Therefore, all challenges to the industrious are burdens to the lazy.

14

Extended arguments, such as those found in editorials, essays, religious and political tracts, and the like, are often difficult to analyze. Not only are premises and conclusions sometimes difficult to identify, but the skeleton of the argument is frequently obscured by rhetorical embellishments, illustrations, explanations, statements of opinion, and emotional appeals, as well as a host of other sorts of expository prose. Extended arguments may consist of a string of subarguments, with conclusions of some subarguments functioning as premises of other subarguments. Premises and conclusions are often suppressed in extended arguments and left for the reader to provide or presuppose. Although there is no simple technique for examining extended argumentation, several devices can be used in an extended argument analysis.

First, is it helpful to number the separate statements in an extended argument; the numbers can then be referenced in order to discuss the statements without undue prolixity. Second, arrows can be inserted to indicate the relation of evidential or inferential support, as follows:

This diagram says that statement ② supports statement ① . Third, braces indicate conjoint **support** either **by** premises or **of** conclusions. Thus the diagram

illustrates that ② and ③ conjointly support ① . The diagram

says, on the other hand, that each of ② and ③ supports ① independently. The diagram

says that ① supports both ② and ③ . It is in fact equivalent to the following pair of diagrams.

A fourth device useful to illustrate the structure of some extended arguments is the equals sign. Thus, the diagram

$$① = ②$$

says that numerals 1 and 2 are attached to essentially the same statement (in technical language: the same proposition).

Sample Exercise from Section 1.6, Part I

① Violence as a way of achieving racial justice is both impractical and immoral. ② It is impractical because ③ it is a descending spiral ending in destruction for all. ④ The old law of an eye for an eye leaves everybody blind. ⑤ It is immoral because ⑥ it seeks to humiliate the opponent rather than win his understanding. ⑦ It seeks to annihilate rather than to convert. ⑧ Violence is immoral because ⑨ it thrives on hatred rather than love. ⑩ It destroys community and makes brotherhood impossible. ⑪ It leaves society in monologue rather than dialogue. ⑫ Violence ends by defeating itself. ⑬ It creates bitterness in the survivor and brutality in the destroyers.

In this argument, ① is clearly the main conclusion. It is a conjunction of two statements, ② and ⑤ . In turn, ⑤ is just the same statement (or: proposition) as ⑧. We may construe that statement ⑬ directly supports ①, since bitterness in the survivor may be viewed as an impracticality, and brutality in the destroyers may be viewed as an immorality. Thus, the passage should be diagrammed as follows:

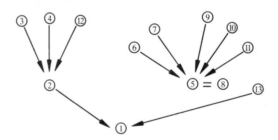

If, instead of ④ being viewed as a different statement from ③ , it is seen as a rhetorically flamboyant version of ③ , then the equals sign may be placed between ③ and ④ and the arrow from ④ to ② ommitted. Additionally, some interpreters may feel that ② and ⑤ should be joined with a brace.

16

Additional Exercises for Section 1.6

Using the devices introduced in this Section, construct diagrams of the following arguments.

1. ① The man who broke into this warehouse must have been rather heavy. ② His footprints sink at least an inch into this dry soil, and ③ his shoe size is at least a thirteen. Moreover, ④ we can see by where he bumped his head on this rafter that he is at least six and a half feet tall.

2. ① The population of the world increases, as Malthus said, far out of proportion to the world's food supply. ② Indeed, it can be maintained that the world's food supply is approaching a theoretical maximum, for ③ the world's arable land is at present nearly all cultivated, and ④ technology promises very little in the way of increasing the land's productivity. It is obvious, therefore, that ⑤ population control is one of the world's most pressing problems.

3. ① Modern war must be total war, for ② modern weaponry demands that battle must be pushed to the technological extreme if it is to be won and ③ no one wages war without the intention to win. But since ④ total war implies total destruction and ⑤ total destruction is incompatible with civilized life, ⑥ pacifism is the only consistent moral and social policy.

4. ① The legacy of the past is the directives of the present. ② Our social ills, as everyone recognizes, are passed from one generation to the next. ③ The means of the present are, however, the hard-won lessons of the past: ④ we ignore history only to repeat it. ⑤ It is clear, then, that a study of history is a prerequisite for a rational life in the present.

5. ① The development of the human fetus from conception to birth is a qualitatively continuous process. ② There are no sudden leaps in either mental or physical fetal maturation. ③ Clearly the end of fetal development is a human being, and ④ the treatment of human beings is clearly the paramount concern of the moral enterprise. Because ⑤ the treatment of human beings is so crucial morally, and because ⑥ no lines can be drawn between what is and is not a human being, ⑦ moral circumspection requires that we treat the fetus in any stage of development as if it were a human being.

2
LANGUAGE, MEANING, AND DEFINITION

2.1 COGNITIVE MEANING AND EMOTIVE MEANING

Ordinary discourse employs language in many ways, but two prominent functions of language are to convey information and to evoke and express emotion. Although few words are used purely to express emotion ("ouch," "damn," when used as an expletive, for example), many words can have both an emotional and cognitive significance. The words "police officer" are perhaps emotively bare or neutral, but "peace officer," while conveying the very same cognitive notion, has a positive or honorific emotional overtone. "Cop," "bull," and "pig" are often used with the same cognitive import but each convey a negative or pejorative emotional overtone.

The fact that many words have emotional meaning as well as cognitive meaning is important for the analysis of argument because an argument may be persuasive, not because of its intrinsic strength, but rather because its emotionally-charged language is appealing. In politics, religion, advertising, and morals, emotionally-invested language is heavily employed; in these areas of discourse especially, one must be on guard to avoid being taken in unawares by intrinsically weak argumentation.

Additional Exercises for Section 2.1

Each of the following words is emotionally charged. Identify, for each, whether the emotional tone is predominantly positive or negative, and replace each with a more or less emotively neutral word.

1. valiant steed
2. broken-down nag
3. shyster
4. quack
5. hag
6. drunkard
7. senior citizen
8. jock
9. man of God
10. trusty firearm

2.2 THE INTENSION AND EXTENSION OF TERMS

A word is a *term* if it may be used as the subject of a statement. Terms consist of proper names, common names, and descriptive phrases. For example, "George Washington," "dog," and "house on the hill" are terms.

Terms have an *intensional meaning* and an *extensional meaning*. The intensional meaning, or *intension*, of a term is the qualities or attributes that the term *connotes* (and for this reason it is also called the *connotation* of the term). Note that in logic "connotation" has a different meaning than it does in linguistics, where "connotation" refers to the subtle nuances of a word. The extensional meaning, or *extension*, of a term is the members of the class of things that the term *denotes* (and for this reason is also called the *denotation* of the term).

A term has *empty extension* if there are no members of the class of things it denotes; for example, the term "werewolf" has empty extension. This is related to the fact that *intension determines extension*: a thing is a member of the class a term denotes if and only if it has the qualities that the term connotes. It follows that there are no meaningful terms with empty intensions—if a term does not connote any qualities at all, it is meaningless, and thus it would be impossible to determine its extension.

Terms may be put in an order: an order of increasing intension, increasing extension, decreasing intension, or decreasing extension. A series of terms is in order of increasing intension when each term in the series (except the first) connotes more qualities than the previous term. A series of terms is in order of increasing extension when each term in the series (except the first) denotes a class that both includes all the members of the class denoted by the previous term and also other things not in that class. The terms "number," "even number," and "even number greater than 2" are in order of increasing intension, while the terms "even number greater than 2," "even number," and "number" are in order of increasing extension. This example illustrates that increasing intension often corresponds with decreasing extension, and vice-versa. But this correspondence is not absolutely necessary or always the case. (See the text for examples in which this correspondence does not obtain.)

Sample Exercises from Exercise 2.2, Part I

1. "Extortion," "practitioner," "seriousness," "scarlet," "reinvest-
    ment," "Thomas Jefferson," "Empire State Building," "graceful
    dancer," "tallest man on the squad," and "mountain top" are clearly
    capable of being used as the subject of a statement; so they are
    clearly terms. "Laborious," "cunningly," "interestingly impas-
    sive," "therefore," "annoy," "render satisfactory," "wake up,"
    "not only," "between," and "since" clearly cannot serve as the
    subject of a statement and so are not terms. "Forever" is defined
    by the dictionary as an adverb, and in this sense it cannot be a
    term. However, "forever" is sometimes used in the sense of "eter-
    nity" ("Forever is a long,long time"), and in this sense it is a
    term. Because the phrase "whoever studies" can be used as the sub-
    ject of a sentence (e.g., "Whoever studies will learn"), it fits the
    criterion for being a term.

2. The following are in order of increasing intension:

    a. Plant, tree, conifer, spruce, Sitka spruce.
    b. Vehicle, car, sports car, Italian sports car, Maserati.
    c. Person, professional person, Doctor of Medicine, surgeon, brain surgeon.
    d. Animal, mammal, marsupial, kangaroo, wallaby.
    e. Polygon, quadrilateral, parallelogram, rectangle, square.

Additional Exercises for Section 2.2

1. Construct a series of four terms of increasing intension.

2. Construct a series of four terms of increasing extension.

3. Construct a series of terms of decreasing intension.

4. Construct a series of terms of decreasing extension.

5. Describe the following series as to intension and extension: implement, farm implement, hoe.

6. Try to give the intension of the following terms: triangle, right triangle, isosceles triangle, equilateral triangle.

7. Identify the extension of each of the following terms: ghost, number that equals its own square, last king of France, rational number whose square is 2, perfect square number between 1 and 100.

8. What elements are common to the intensions of the following pairs of terms?

    a. square, triangle   c. horse, cow
    b. square, equilateral triangle   d. chair, book

9. Give five terms with empty extension.

10. Give five terms whose extension consists of exactly one item.

Definitions are intended to explicate the meanings of words. Every definition consists of a *definiendum* (the word or group of words that is supposed to be defined by the definition) and a *definiens* (the word or group of words that does the defining). The definiens symbolizes the same meaning as the definiendum. Definitions may be of various types. A *stipulative definition* assigns a meaning to a word for the first time. (The word may already have other standard meanings, but the stipulative definition assigns a new meaning to the word.) This assignment, though there may be some rationale for it, is essentially arbitrary: it is independent of any prior meanings the word may have had. Consequently, there is no such thing as a true or false stipulative definition. A *lexical definition* is used to report the meaning or meanings that a word already has. Dictionaries consist of lexical definitions. Accordingly, a lexical definition, unlike a stipulative definition, can be true or false: it is true if it correctly reports the meaning the word already has; otherwise, it is false.
Another sort of definition is the *precising definition*, which has the purpose of reducing the vagueness of a word. (Vagueness must be distinguished from ambiguity: a word is *vague* if it is not clear just what the word means in every case; a word is *ambiguous* if it has two or more distinct, clear meanings. For example, "democracy" is vague, while "saw"—which can mean both the past tense of "see" and the wood-cutting tool—is ambiguous or at least is susceptible to ambiguous usage.) Precising definitions are often found, for example, in legal texts. Like stipulative definitions, precising definitions involve a new assignment of meaning; but, unlike stipulative definitions, precising definitions do not assign meaning arbitrarily.
Theoretical definitions provide theoretical characterizations of the things denoted by their definienda. They provide ways of conceiving those things that have deductive consequences in the theory at hand. The definition of "work" as "force multiplied by the distance over which the force is exerted" is a theoretical definition used in physics. Not all theoretical definitions occur in science; some, for example, occur in philosophy, art criticism, and other theoretical disciplines. Like stipulative definitions, theoretical definitions are neither true nor false, at least not in any simple sense of these terms.
Persuasive definitions have the purpose of creating a favorable or unfavorable attitude toward the thing or things denoted by their definienda. Persuasive definitions are offered as if they were merely lexical definitions, but they contain value-laden elements that are intended to have a persuasive effect. "Democracy is the governing of responsible people by themselves" is a persuasive definition that is designed to engender a positive attitude; "democracy is the rule of the mob" is a persuasive definition that is designed to engender a negative attitude.

Additional Exercises for Section 2.3

1. Invent opposing pairs of persuasive definitions for "religion."

2. How would you characterize the definition of "entropy" found in thermodynamics?

3. A mathematician defines a "group" as "a set of objects together with a binary relation, such that the set contains an identity element, the set is closed under the binary relation, every element of the set has an inverse in the set, and the binary relation is associative." What sort of definition is this?

4. "Death is the moment of the soul's liberation, the healing of the disease of life." What sort of definition is this?

5. "A lime is a small greenish citrus fruit, shaped like a lemon but usually smaller than a lemon." What sort of definition is this?

2.4 DEFINITIONAL TECHNIQUES

Techniques used to produce definitions may be classified into extensional techniques and intensional techniques. An *extensional definition* is one that assigns a meaning to a word by indicating the class of things that the definiendum denotes. An *intensional definition* is one that assigns a meaning to a word by indicating the qualities or attributes that the definiendum connotes.

Extensional definitions are of at least three types. A *demonstrative*, or *ostensive*, *definition* indicates the members of the definiendum's denotation by *pointing* to them. An *enumerative definition* indicates the members of the definiendum's denotation by *naming* them. A *definition by subclass* indicates the members of the definiendum's denotation by *naming subclasses* of this denotation. Extensional definitions are chiefly used as lexical or stipulative definitions. The main fault of extensional definitions is that they cannot guarantee that the intensional meaning of the definiendum is communicated.

Intensional definitions are also of at least three types. In a *synonymous definition*, the definiens is a single word that connotes the very same attributes as the definiendum. An example is "A physician is a doctor." An *operational definition* assigns a meaning to a word by specifying experimental procedures that can be used to determine whether or not the definiendum applies to any given thing. An example is "A substance is a conductor if and only if, when a battery is connected to the ends of it, a nearby galvanometer deflects." A *definition by genus and difference* assigns a meaning to a term by specifying a genus word and one or more specific-difference words, which together provide the attributes that the definiendum connotes. In logic "genus" simply means a class, and "species" means a smaller subclass of a genus. A specific difference of a species is an attribute that distinguishes that species from other species in the genus. Thus, a species is indicated by giving its genus and its specific difference. If we define "foal" as a newborn horse, then we are employing a definition by genus and difference: the genus is "horse," and the specific difference is "newborn."

Additional Exercises for Section 2.4

1. Construct a definition by genus and difference of "square," "circle," "even number," and "odd number."

2. How would you characterize the following definition: "An object A is heavier than an object B if and only if, whenever A and B are

22

placed in two dishes of a balance scale, A sinks and B
rises."

3. What sort of definition is "An insect is an ant, a grasshopper, a
butterfly, and so on"?

4. What sort of definition is "The color red is *that* color" (said while
pointing to a certain color)?

5. Provide operational definitions for "ductile" and "malleable."

6. Give definitions by subclass for "marsupial" and "ungulate."

7. Can theoretical and stipulative definitions always be sharply
distinguished?

8. Provide a definition for "junior college." What type is it?

9. Construct an enumerative definition of "planet."

10. What sort of definition is "A tenant is a dweller"?

2.5 CRITERIA FOR LEXICAL DEFINITIONS

The purpose of a lexical definition is to report the meaning a word has
as it is actually used in a language. Lexical definitions may achieve
this purpose to a greater or lesser degree. The following rules help
evaluate lexical definitions.

Rule 1: A lexical definition should conform to the rules of proper
grammar.

Rule 2: A lexical definition should convey the *essential* meaning
of the word being defined. The attributes mentioned in the definition
should be the important or necessary features of the thing defined, not
trivial ones.

Rule 3: A lexical definition should be neither *too broad* nor *too
narrow*. A definition is too broad if the definiens applies to things
other than the things that are being defined. For instance, "A fish is
a creature that swims in the ocean" is too broad because it includes
whales and dolphins, which are not fish. A definition is too narrow if
it does not apply to all the things that are being defined. For instance,
the above definition of "fish" is too narrow because it does not apply to
freshwater fish. Thus, a definition can be both too broad and too narrow.

Rule 4: A lexical definition must not be *circular*. A circular
definition uses the definiendum in some way in the definiens and is thus
not genuinely informative.

Rule 5: A lexical definition should not be *negative* when it can be
affirmative. Nevertheless, some words, like "pristine" and "virginity,"
are intrinsically negative; for them, a negative definition is quite
appropriate.

Rule 6: A lexical definition should not be expressed in figurative,
obscure, vague, or ambiguous language.

Rule 7: A lexical definition should avoid *affective terminology*.

Rule 8: A lexical definition should indicate the *context* to which the definiens pertains. For example, "mate" has one meaning in the context of a game of chess and quite another in the context of sailing.

Sample Exercises from Exercise 2.5

1. A sculpture is a three-dimensional image made of marble.

   This definition is too narrow in that it does not include sculptures made of iron, brass, or other materials.

2. "Elusory" means elusive.

   This definition is circular.

3. "Develop" means to transform by the action of chemicals.

   This definition fails to indicate the context (photography) to which the definiens pertains.

4. A cynic is a person who knows the price of everything and the value of nothing. —*Oscar Wilde*

   This definition makes use of sarcastic language. In addition, its use of the word "value" is vague.

Additional Exercises for Section 2.5

Use the seven rules for evaluating lexical definitions to criticize the following definitions.

1. A pony is a horse.

2. A horse is a large four-legged animal that is ridden and used to do work.

3. A flush is five cards of the same suit.

4. A table is a piece of furniture with four legs and a flat top.

5. A poem is a soul's prayer to reality.

6. A communist is a power-monger with a golden tongue.

7. The soul is the harmony of the body.

8. Knowledge is true belief.

9. Truth is a correspondence between an idea and the way things are.

10. A ball is a spheroid of nonutilitarian functionality.

3
INFORMAL FALLACIES

3.1 FALLACIES IN GENERAL

A *fallacy* is a certain kind of defect in an argument. Fallacies are usually divided into two types: formal and informal. A *formal fallacy* is a fallacy that may be identified by a mere inspection of the form of the argument. An argument having an invalid form, such as "All A are B; all A are C; therefore, all B are C," contains a formal fallacy. An *informal fallacy* is a fallacy that, in order to be identified, requires an analysis of the content of the argument and not just an inspection of its form. For example, "Ronald Reagan is no friend of mine; no friend of mine is a Russian communist; therefore, Ronald Reagan is a Russian communist," may appear to have a valid form, but it is clearly fallacious. Because detecting the fallaciousness of this argument depends on understanding its content—in particular the meaning of "no friend of mine"—the argument contains an informal fallacy.

Informal fallacies may be classified in a number of ways, and it would be presumptuous to claim that any particular classification is complete. The classification in the text contains twenty-two informal fallacies, divided into four groups: fallacies of relevance, fallacies of presumption, fallacies of ambiguity, and fallacies of grammatical analogy.

Exercises for Section 3.1

Try to identify the reason or reasons why each of the following arguments is fallacious.

1. Abortion is miscarriage. Abortion is also a matter of justice. Therefore, abortion is a miscarriage of justice.

2. Sloppy Joe's has the most eaten hamburgers in town. So don't go to Sloppy Joe's for a hamburger: you are likely to find a bite out of it.

3. You will find that if you kill a toad by the light of the full moon, any wart you have will sooner or later go away. So killing a toad by the light of the full moon is a cure for warts.

4. Fagin is a superb thief. Any thief is a man. It follows that Fagin is a superb man.

5. John is heavy-hearted today, so even if you are strong you probably will not be able to lift him.

3.2 FALLACIES OF RELEVANCE

The *fallacies of relevance* apply to arguments with premises that are not logically relevant to the conclusion but that are *psychologically* relevant to the conclusion in such a way as to make the conclusion *seem* to follow from them. In this section ten fallacies of relevance are presented. Section 3.4 discusses others.

1. The *appeal to force* (*argumentum ad baculum*) occurs when the arguer, instead of providing genuine evidence for a conclusion, provides some sort of threat of harm to the listener or reader if the conclusion is not accepted.
2. The *appeal to pity* (*argumentum ad misericordiam*) occurs when the arguer, instead of providing genuine evidence for a conclusion, attempts to get the conclusion accepted by evoking pity from the listener or reader.
3. The *appeal to the people* (*argumentum ad populum*) occurs when the arguer, instead of providing genuine evidence for a conclusion, tries to get the conclusion accepted by playing upon the listener's or reader's desire to be loved, esteemed, admired, valued, recognized, or accepted by others. In the *direct approach*, the arguer tries to get a conclusion accepted by whipping up the collective enthusiasm of a crowd. In the *indirect approach*, the arguer directs the appeal to one or more individuals, concentrating on some aspect of their relation to a crowd or populace. The indirect approach includes the *bandwagon argument* (urging that someone "jump on the bandwagon" so as not to be "left out" or "different"), the *appeal to vanity*, and the *appeal to snobbery*.
4. The *argument against the person* (*argumentum ad hominem*) occurs when one arguer directs his or her attention to the person of a second arguer and not to the second arguer's argument or position. The argument against the person occurs in three forms. In the *ad hominem abusive*, an arguer responds to another person's argument by verbally abusing or attacking that other person. In the *ad hominem circumstantial*, an arguer attempts to discredit his or her opponent's argument or position by calling attention to certain circumstances that affect the opponent, such as ways the opponent's self-interest is served by arguing as he or she does. In the *tu quoque* ("you too") type of ad hominem, the arguer attempts to defend himself or herself by alleging that the opponent is just as guilty. The *tu quoque* is sometimes called the "two wrongs make a right" fallacy.
5. The *appeal to authority* (*argumentum ad verecundiam*) occurs when an arguer cites the testimony or belief of an authority who is not necessarily reliable or who is not an expert in the subject at hand. Citing a legitimate, reliable authority is not committing this fallacy (although such a citation cannot ever amount to a valid deductive argument).
6. The *appeal to ignorance* (*argumentum ad ignorantiam*) occurs in an argument when the premises state that nothing is known with certainty about a certain subject, and the conclusion states something definite about that subject. A typical use of the appeal to ignorance is to argue that because a certain thesis has not been proven, the opposite of that thesis must be true. This fallacy is not committed, however, if the premises state that qualified researchers in the subject at hand have failed after extensive attempts to demonstrate something, and the

26

conclusion states that what they have attempted to demonstrate is not so. Also, this fallacy is not committed in the special context of the courtroom, where a defendant is presumed innocent until proven guilty.

7. The fallacy of *accident* is committed when a general rule is wrongly or unjustifiably applied to a specific case. For example, "Dogs have four legs; Fido just had one of his legs amputated; so Fido is not a dog any more," is a case of accident. The fallacy of accident often occurs in the context of morality, when general moral principles are hastily applied to specific cases. Here is an example: "Thou shalt not kill; therefore, it is morally wrong to use insecticides."

8. The fallacy of *hasty generalization* (*converse accident*) is committed when a conclusion is drawn about all the members of a group or population from premises about some sample of the group that is not representative. A sample is not usually representative if it is too small or is not randomly selected.

9. The fallacy of *false cause* occurs when the link between premises and conclusion in an argument depends on the supposition of some causal connection that does not in fact exist. One variety of the false cause fallacy occurs when it is concluded that one type of event causes another just because events of the first type are regularly followed by events of the second type. This is called *post hoc ergo propter hoc* ("after this therefore because of this"); an example would be to conclude that my watch's coming around to 5:00 or 6:00 A.M. causes the sun to rise. Another variety of the false cause fallacy, called *non causa pro causa* ("not the cause for the cause"), occurs when something taken to be a cause is not a cause at all and the mistake is based on something other than temporal succession.

10. The *fallacy of missing the point* (*ignoratio elenchi*) occurs when the premises of an argument lead, or seem to lead, to one conclusion and then a completely different conclusion is drawn. This fallacy often occurs when, in the course of discussing one issue, an arguer begins to argue about an entirely different (though somehow related) issue. It also occurs when an arguer draws a conclusion that goes far beyond anything for which he or she has provided evidence.

Sample Exercises from Exercise 3.2, Part I

1. Professor Glazebrook's theory about the origin of Martian craters is undoubtedly true. Rudolf Orkin, the great concert pianist, announced his support of the theory in this morning's newspaper.

    This argument is an appeal to authority. There is no reason to think that Rudolf Orkin should be a reliable authority on the subject of Martian craters.

2. Whoever thrusts a knife into another person should be arrested. But surgeons do precisely this when operating. Therefore, surgeons should be arrested.

    This argument commits the fallacy of accident. The general rule stated in the premise should be understood not to apply to the case of surgeons doing their legitimate work.

3. There are more churches in New York City than in any other city in the nation, and more crimes are committed in New York City than anywhere else. So, if we are to eliminate crime, we must abolish the churches.

This argument commits the fallacy of false cause—*non causa pro causa* variety. The conclusion depends on the supposition that the presence of churches causes crime.

4. Susanna's dentist advised her to have extensive work done on her teeth. This advice should not be taken seriously, however, because if she has this work done, the dentist will receive an excellent fee.

    This argument commits the fallacy ad hominem circumstantial. It attempts to discredit the dentist's advice by calling attention to the circumstances in which the dentist gives it and more specifically by suggesting that the advice is in the dentist's own self-interest.

Additional Exercises for Section 3.2

Identify the fallacies of relevance in the following arguments.

1. Mary must have ESP: last night she had a weird dream about her mother and this morning her mother had a heart attack.

2. Fifty million Americans have tried Brand X cigarettes. You should try them, too.

3. Ninety-five percent of heroin addicts smoked marijuana before they became addicted to herion. It is obvious that marijuana leads to heroin addiction.

4. This logic course has caused me a lot of trouble, so I'll never take a course in philosophy again.

5. Women are genetically determined to be, on the average, smaller and weaker than men. They are just naturally different. It follows that the whole idea of the ERA is, in the nature of things, ridiculous.

6. Life is precious; it is really the supreme moral value. So it is clear that abortion is morally wrong.

7. Women certainly have a right to do what they want with their very own bodies. So it is clear that abortion is morally allowable.

8. Vava Voom has been arguing on national television that Americans should send relief packages to starving children in poor countries. But no one should be convinced by her—after all, Miss Voom is nothing but a cheap actress who works in porno films.

9. Republicans have been arguing that massive tax cuts to business and industry are necessary to get the economy back into a healthy state. But in considering their program, just remember that the Republicans are precisely the business people and industrialists who will most immediately benefit from such a tax cut.

10. No less a person than General M. A. Sidewinder supports this bond issue, so it must be good for our educational system.

11. There can't be anything very wrong with stealing from your employer, since nearly everyone does it.

12. No one has found all the links in the supposed chain from one-celled animals to human beings. Therefore, the theory of evolution is nothing but a myth.

13. We should not dismiss Mr. Writeoff from the vice-presidency; after all, he was an orphan and has been crippled for several years.

14. If you students don't think you should invite me to the class party, just reflect that I still have not turned in the grades for the class.

15. The 1960s were the heyday of permissive childrearing, and today in the 1980s we have the highest crime rate among people in their twenties that the United States has ever had. We must return to strict and severe child raising if we want to prevent the crime rate from going even higher.

16. After many years of writing philosophy, Freidrich Nietzsche went mad. That shows the dangerous nature of the subject.

17. No one has ever seen, heard, or talked with God. It follows that God just does not exist at all.

18. You say you object to the American foreign policy in Europe. You ought to go become a citizen of Russia then.

19. Gentlemen, the dean has accused our department of irresponsibility in managing our budget. But I happen to know that the dean over-spent his own budget this year in every category.

20. Don't be just a face in the crowd. Wear FineFare shirts and jeans.

3.3 FALLACIES OF PRESUMPTION, AMBIGUITY, AND GRAMMATICAL ANALOGY

The *fallacies of presumption* include begging the question and complex question. In both these fallacies the premises presume what they purport to prove. (See Section 3.4 for another fallacy of presumption.)

11. The fallacy of *begging the question* (*petitio principii*) occurs when the arguer uses some trick or device to hide the fact that a premise may not be true. When this fallacy is committed, the argument must be valid, one premise must be questionable, and some artifice must be employed to hide the questionable status of the premise in question. One typical way of begging the question is to present a premise that more or less has the same meaning as the conclusion but is worded differently. Begging the question has also been called circular reasoning.

12. The fallacy of *complex question* occurs when an apparently single question is asked that really involves two or more questions, all of which are answered by an appropriate answer to the apparently single question. Such a question is the familiar "Have you stopped beating your wife?" which involves the two questions "Did you ever beat your wife?"

29

and "If you did ever beat your wife, have you stopped?" The complex
question, although not itself an argument, is such that the question,
taken together with an answer to it, yields an argument that establishes
the truth of the proposition presupposed in the question. Thus, the
proposition presupposed in the question "Have you stopped beating your
wife?" is "You once did beat your wife," and whether the person answers
yes or no to the question the truth of this proposition will be implied.

The *fallacies of ambiguity* include equivocation and amphiboly. In both
cases the faultiness of the argument arises because of some ambiguity in
either the premises or conclusion or both.

13. The fallacy of *equivocation* occurs when the inference in an
argument depends on the fact that a word or phrase is used in two or more
different senses. For example, "Banks have lots of money in them; the
sides of rivers are banks; therefore, the sides of rivers have lots of
money in them," is an argument in which the inference depends on the
word "banks," which is equivocated upon (used with different senses) in
the argument.

14. The fallacy of *amphiboly* occurs when an arguer, beginning with
some statement that is ambiguous owing to a structural (grammatical)
defect, proceeds to interpret it in a way in which it was not intended
and to draw a conclusion based on this faulty interpretation. The original statement is usually made by someone other than the arguer. The
structural defect is often a mistake in grammar or punctuation, such as
dangling modifiers, confusion of restrictive and nonrestrictive clauses
and phrases, and ambiguous reference of pronoun to antecedent. A well-
known example of amphiboly is Groucho Marx's classic "One morning I shot
an elephant in my pajamas. How he got into my pajamas I'll never know."

The main difference between amphiboly and equivocation is that in
amphiboly the ambiguity is traceable to a *structural* defect in a *statement*, whereas in equivocation the ambiguity is traceable to a *word* that
has two or more distinct senses. If the ambiguity in an argument can be
removed by a structural or grammatical alteration, such as a change in
punctuation or a rearrangement of words, it is an amphiboly. If the
ambiguity is removable only by a substitution of different terms, it is
probably an equivocation.

The *fallacies of grammatical analogy* include composition, division,
and false analogy. In these fallacies arguments are employed which,
though faulty, are grammatically analogous to other arguments that are
unimpeachable. The similarity in linguistic structure makes the fallacious argument appear good. In composition and division the faultiness
in the argument arises because an attribute or characteristic is improperly
transferred from parts of a whole to the whole or from the whole itself to
its parts. The whole in question might be a physical whole composed of
physical parts, a class composed of members, or a species composed of the
entities it comprises. Of special relevance to the fallacies of grammatical analogy is the difference between *distributive* and *collective*
predication.of an attribute. An attribute is predicated distributively
if it is meant to apply to each and every one of the members of the group.
An attribute is predicated collectively if it is meant to apply to the
group taken as a whole. "Whooping cranes are scarce" is, for example, a
collective prediction--it does not mean that each whooping crane is
scarce. Shifting illegitimately between distributive and collective
predications of an attribute is one form of the fallacies of grammatical
analogy.

30

15. The fallacy of *composition* occurs when the inference in an argument depends on the erroneous transference of a characteristic from the parts of something to the whole. For instance, going from a distributive predication to the corresponding collective predication is one sort of fallacy of composition. Another would be going from the characteristics of the elements of a chemical compound to the characteristics of the compound ("Hydrogen and oxygen are gases; therefore, H_2O is a gas"). Not every instance of transferring characteristics from parts to wholes is illegitimate, so not every instance of such transference is a fallacy of composition.

16. The fallacy of *division* occurs when the inference in an argument depends on the erroneous transference of a characteristic from a whole to some one or more of its parts. Division is the exact reverse of composition.

Composition and division are sometimes confused with hasty generalization and accident, respectively. Composition can be distinguished from hasty generalization as follows: in hasty generalization, the conclusion is not an assertion about a group taken as a whole (a collective predication); rather, it is an assertion about all (each and every one of) the members of a group (a distributive predication). But in composition the assertion in the conclusion is a collective predication. Similarly, division can be distinguished from accident as follows: in accident the inference is from a general assertion (a distributive predication) to a specific assertion, but in division the inference is from an assertion about a group taken as a whole (a collective predication) to an assertion about the members of the group.

17. False Dichotomy. A dichotomy is a pair of alternatives (states, characteristics, or conditions) that are both mutually exclusive and jointly exhaustive. A pair X, Y is mutually exclusive if nothing can be both X and Y; it is jointly exhaustive if everything must be either X or Y. A false dichotomy is a pair of alternatives, presented as if it were a dichotomy when it is not in fact a dichotomy. The *fallacy of false dichotomy* is committed when an argument rests for its goodness on presenting some pair of conditions as if it were a dichotomy when it is not. The usual method is to present a false dichotomy in a premise with the *either...or* form, known as a disjunctive premise. The argument then proceeds fallaciously in one of two ways. First, one of the alternatives is denied and the other is concluded to. When the alternatives are not jointly exhaustive (or in other words, when the disjunctive premise is simply not true), this procedure is fallacious, though the argument looks like the valid argument form known as disjunctive syllogism. Second, one of the alternatives is affirmed and the denial of the other is concluded to. When the alternatives are not mutually exclusive, this procedure is fallacious, though the argument looks like a valid argument form using the so-called "exclusive *or*."

Sample Exercises from Exercise 3.3, Part I

1. George said that he was interviewing for a job drilling oil wells in the supervisor's office. I conclude that the supervisor must have an awfully messy office.

   This argument is an instance of amphiboly. The ambiguity concerns whether "in the supervisor's office" modifies "interviewing" or "drilling." The defect is thus structural and may be removed by relocating the modifying phrase.

31

2. All men are mortal. Therefore, some day man will disappear from the earth.

This argument commits the fallacy of composition: it illegitimately transfers a property (mortality) from the members of a class (the class of men) to the class itself (man).

3. Are you still drinking excessively?

This is a complex question. The two questions involved in it are "Have you ever drunk excessively?" and "If you have ever drunk excessively, are you still doing so?" Either a yes or a no answer would enable an argument to be constructed with the conclusion "You have drunk excessively."

4. Picasso is the greatest artist of the twentieth century. We know this is so because certain art critics have described him in these terms. These art critics are correct in their assessment because they have a more keenly developed sense of appreciation than the average critic. This is true because it takes a more keenly developed sense of appreciation to realize that Picasso is the greatest artist of the twentieth century.

This argument commits the fallacy of begging the question. The arguer tricks the reader or listener into accepting the doubtful conclusion by hiding it as one of the premises in a long chain of premises.

Additional Exercises for Section 3.3

Identify the fallacies of presupposition, ambiguity, and grammatical analogy in the following arguments.

1. Almost every person in the U.S. has two arms. That alone shows the tremendous need for gun control laws in this country.

2. Weeds are plentiful this year. Therefore, this particular dandelion is plentiful this year.

3. Children should be seen and not heard. This is obvious because only adults should be both seen and heard.

4. The news said that, waving majestically in the breeze Victoria saw the Stars and Stripes. I wonder if she would notice the flag if she stopped behaving so haughtily.

5. The reporter said that, stepping up to the podium, John cleared his throat and delivered a two-hour extemporaneous address. It must have taken John a long time to step up to that podium.

6. *Al*: Do you make a lot of profit on your narcotics sales?
   Betty: No!
   Al: So you do indeed sell narcotics.

7. *Political ad:* You can either vote for me or else commit this nation to slavery at the hands of the Soviet Union by 1987.

32

8. *News item*: The stealthy reconnaissance agent spied the giant Russian weapons factory hiding in a small clump of grass.
    Reader: Those Russians really are advanced, getting that entire factory hidden in that grass.

9. *Sign*: Eat at Sloppy Joe's and you'll never eat anyplace else again.
    Patron: Sloppy Joe must be seasoning his burgers with arsenic these days.

10. Joe told his worst enemy, Sam, that he was a swine. Joe must have a lot of character to make an admission like that to his own worst enemy.

11. John sat absolutely glued to his seat during the movie. He must have had a lot of trouble getting unstuck when the show ended.

12. Auto thefts are occurring at an alarming rate this month. It must be technology that is enabling thieves to carry out such speedy robberies.

13. It says here on the sports page that the Boosters' Club had seasoned Coach Passa Bomb at its annual awards banquet. It looks like cannibalism has finally broken out openly among the boosters.

14. I've heard that 55 percent of all Americans are fat. But that can't be right: I'm sure that no more than 40 percent of me is fat.

15. A cat or dog has the attribute of normalcy only if it has four legs. It follows that a bird or a man has the property of normalcy only if it has four legs.

16. All pieces of chalk are white. It follows that the class of all pieces of chalk is white.

17. John said that he smoked his pipes and listened with both ears. John must have looked pretty strange with those pipes in his ears.

18. The real numbers are continuous, and the number one is a real number. So the number one is continuous.

19. Strauss's tunes are very light, so probably even a little child could carry them.

20. Cells are tiny. An elephant is nothing but cells. So an elephant is tiny.

3.4 FALLACIES IN ORDINARY LANGUAGE

In this section five additional fallacies are presented. Like the seventeen fallacies we have examined so far, they may be classified under the general headings already defined. Weak analogy, slippery slope, straw man, and red herring are fallacies of relevance; suppressed evidence is a fallacy of presumption. These five fallacies are presented separately because they are typically more difficult to detect and to identify than the other seventeen.

18. The fallacy of weak *analogy* occurs in inductive arguments from analogy when the analogy between two things is not strong enough to support the conclusion. The basic form of an argument from analogy is

Entity A has attributes a, b, c, d, and z.
Entity B has attributes a, b, c, and d.
Therefore, entity B probably has attribute z, too.

For this to be a strong inductive argument, there must be some systematic (causal) connection between possession of the attributes a through d and possession of the attribute z. If such a systematic connection does not exist, the argument is weak and commits the fallacy of weak analogy.

19. The fallacy of *slippery slope* is a variety of the false cause fallacy. It occurs when the conclusion of an argument depends on the claim that a certain event or situation will initiate a more or less long chain of events leading to some undesirable consequence, and when there is not sufficient reason to think that the chain of events will actually take place.

20. The fallacy of *suppressed evidence* is a fallacy of presumption that is closely related to begging the question. It consists in passing off what are at best half-truths as if they were the whole truth and using them as premises in an argument. This fallacy is also committed if an arguer presents the premises in such a way as to imply that they are the only facts relevant to the conclusion when in fact there are other relevant facts that point in the opposite direction. One example of such a fallacy is, "You ought to become a Hollywood starlet; starlets are so glamorous, they make money easily, and they quickly rise to full-fledged stardom."

21. The fallacy of *straw man* occurs when an arguer misinterprets a certain argument or position for the purpose of more easily attacking it, refutes the misinterpreted argument or position (which is known as the "straw man" that the arguer has "set up"), and then concludes that the real argument or position has been refuted. The following argument against freedom of speech commits the straw man fallacy."

Freedom of speech is not nearly as desirable as some people think. Why should anyone be allowed, for example, to incite others to violence, to make threatening phone calls, or to shout obscenities at policemen? And surely no one thinks people should be allowed to make fraudulent proposals, or to reveal military secrets to our enemies.

The real issue in freedom of speech is, of course, quite different from what this argument suggests.

22. The *red herring* fallacy is similar to the fallacy of missing the point. It occurs when an arguer diverts the attention of the reader or listener by going off on extraneous issues and points but ends by assuming that some conclusion relevant to the point at hand has been established. In the red herring fallacy, the argumentation seems to have the purpose of throwing the reader or listener off the right track. In missing the point, the argument points clearly to some conclusion, but that conclusion is not the same as the one at issue; in the red herring fallacy, the argument usually does not point clearly to any conclusion.

Sample Exercises from Exercise 3.4, Part I

1. A number of pursuasive arguments have been advanced in favor of the
    unification of Ireland. But if all the Protestants in the north
    are forced to become Catholic, this will only increase the tensions
    and hatred. Surely, if anything is true a person should have the
    right to practice the religion of his or her choice. Thus, in
    light of these facts it appears that the arguments in favor of
    unification are not so good after all.

    This argument commits the fallacy of straw man. The real issue is
    the unification of Ireland, not the forced conversion of Protestants
    to Catholicism.

2. General American Savings and Loan is a great place to put your
    money. For a $1,000 minimum balance you receive a checking account
    with no service charges, and for an additional $1,000 they give
    you a free safety deposit box. On top of that you receive $5\frac{1}{4}$ per-
    cent interest on your deposit, and every account is insured for up
    to $100,000.

    This argument, like many advertisements, commits the fallacy of
    suppressed evidence. Not mentioned are the prevailing interest
    rates. If they are substantially higher than $5\frac{1}{4}$ percent, a person
    could get a much better return on his or her money by placing it
    elsewhere, such as in a money market fund. Moreover, the savings
    and loan company will use the money deposited with it to invest
    at the prevailing interest rates. Thus, it is at best a half-truth
    to say that the checking account has no service charge and that the
    safety deposit box is free.

Additional Exercises for Section 3.4

Identify the fallacies of ordinary language in the following arguments.

1. If we do not match the Russians gun for gun and missile for missile,
    their agressive adventurism will soon spread from Eastern Europe
    and Afghanistan to the Middle East. Eventually we'll be facing
    them at the borders of Canada and Mexico.

2. The Roman Empire, poised at the height of its power but eaten up
    by internal moral decay, had only a few years of political integrity
    left to it, though none of its contemporary citizens realized that
    gloomy fact. The moral for our nation is obvious.

3. Today's youth are callow and insensitive. Why, my Aunt Emma has
    spent years trying to get the young people of her neighborhood
    interested in proper diet. She marches up and down the street
    handing out, free mind you, dietary plans to any teenager who will
    take them. But do you think they are interested? They just stuff
    their faces with cola and chips and go on their way.

4. Auto racing is the sport for you. It's fun, it's challenging, and
    it's exciting.

5. I don't know why people still bring up the subject of Hiroshima. We dropped a bomb, and it destroyed some buildings and killed some people. But that's to be expected in a war.

6. This animal has four legs, hair, and a tail. Therefore, we can reasonably expect that it will have a diet similar to that of a horse.

7. At LeMon Auto Sales every used car on our lot has been individually inspected by Mr. LeMon himself. He makes sure that every car we offer to the public meets his own personal standards. That's why it makes good sense to buy at LeMon.

8. Unless we maintain severe penalties for possession of small amounts of marijuana, it's inevitable that penalties for possession of large amounts of the drug will eventually be lowered. After that, the penalties for possessing hard drugs will become lighter. We can expect that hallucinogens and opiates will become as common on our streets as candy.

9. The universe is like a giant organism, with parts mutually inter-locking like tissues and organs. We may conclude, then, that its origin is biological and begin our search for its parents.

10. A household that fails to maintain a balanced budget will eventually go bankrupt. Now consider a government that has a consistent policy of deficit spending, maintained over many years. Like the household, it must eventually go bankrupt.

11. Just allow prosecutors to reintroduce evidence obtained via a tech-nical error in procedure, and pretty soon judges will be allowing evidence obtained via substantial illegality in conduct. Then the entire Fourth Amendment will be rendered in effect null and void.

12. Coeducational dormitories must be stopped at all costs. No parent wants to send a son or daughter to school and have that son or daughter forced to submit to the invasion of every aspect of pri-vacy.

13. It's obvious that the educational philosophy of our decade has gone astray. Students are late to classes, they have no sense of disci-pline, and they like blue jeans and T-shirts better than coats and ties. Why, today people don't even care enough about our education-al programs to attend PTA meetings. If a student is spanked, some lawyer immediately hauls a teacher into court. Lawyers are much too powerful anyway.

14. There can be no doubt that communists are infiltrating everywhere. Even the local public library recently sponsored an evening lecture on transcendental meditation. ERA activists hand out fliers in one of our local shopping malls, and the Hari Krishnas solicit donations at the airport. I don't know why we tolerate this sort of thing. The city council should levy a fine against all public loiterers. The city council has been so ineffective in recent years. The weak city council is the basic reason for the spread of communism in our city.

15. The objective historian must admit that Adolf Hitler was an admirable national leader. He solved Germany's economic problems, he restored the patriotic pride of nearly every German citizen, and he reinstituted order and discipline in public life. He made Germany into a nation that other nations could ignore no longer.

16. Football must go at this university. The student body just cannot tolerate these recruiting scandals and the extra privileges accorded to scholarship athletes.

17. Soccer and football are both played on a large field with a ball that is often kicked in the course of the game. It follows that the typical good football player would make a good soccer player.

18. My last cocker spaniel was a parti-colored female and she was an excellent hunter. It follows that this parti-colored cocker female will be an excellent hunter, too.

19. I bought XYZ stock last year after a long decline in the market, and made a nice profit on it when the market went back up. So, since the market has again been on a long decline, I ought to buy XYZ stock again.

20. A guest-worker program for foreign nationals would be a disaster for this country. Every country in the world would have its citizens clamoring for admission to the U.S.A. The prospect of paying them cheap wages would encourage businesses to entice them here. Foreign nationals would collect in ghettos, and pretty soon we would have pockets of foreigners in our midst, speaking their own languages and practicing their own customs. These would become pockets of crime and the victim would be the average law-abiding U.S. citizen.

4
CATEGORICAL PROPOSITIONS

4.1 THE COMPONENTS OF CATEGORICAL PROPOSITIONS

A *categorical proposition* is a proposition that relates two classes, or categories, denoted respectively by the *subject term* and the *predicate term*. The categorical proposition asserts that either all or part of the class denoted by the subject term is either included in or excluded from the class denoted by the predicate term. There are thus four basic types of categorical proposition, and each type can be put into one of the following four standard forms:

> All *S* are *P*.
> No *S* are *P*.
> Some *S* are *P*.
> Some *S* are not *P*.

In these forms, *S* stands for the subject term and *P* for the predicate term. The words "all," "no," and "some" are called logical *quantifiers*. (Note that "some" is understood to have the meaning "at least one."). The words "are" and "are not" are called *copulas*.

Sample Exercises from Exercise 4.1

1. Some pigs are wild animals.

   quantifier: Some
   subject term: pigs
   copula: are
   predicate term: wild animals

2. No canaries are melancholy creatures.

   quantifier: No
   subject term: canaries
   copula: are
   predicate term: melancholy creatures

In class notation "All S are P" means that every member of the S class is a member of the P class. "No S are P" means that no member of the S class is a member of the P class. "Some S are P" means that at least one member of the S class is a member of the P class. "Some S are not P" means that at least one member of the S class is not a member of the P class. The *quality* of a categorical proposition is defined as *affirmative* if it affirms class membership (as do "All S are P" and "Some S are P") and *negative* if it denies class membership (as do "No S are P" and "Some S are not P"). The *quantity* of a categorical proposition is defined as *universal* if it makes a claim about every member of the S class (as do "All S are P" and "No S are P") and *particular* if it makes a claim about just some (at least one) member of the S class (as do "Some S are P" and "Some S are not P").

The universal affirmative categorical proposition ("All S are P") is known as an A proposition; the universal negative categorical proposition ("No S are P") is known as an E proposition; the particular affirmative categorical proposition ("Some S are P") is known as an I proposition; and the particular negative categorical proposition ("Some S are not P") is known as an O proposition.

The *distribution* of a term (either S or P) in a categorical proposition is defined as follows. A term is *distributed* in a proposition if and only if that proposition makes a claim about every member of the class denoted by that term; otherwise, the term is *undistributed* in the proposition. Clearly the S term in an A proposition is distributed. The P term in an A proposition is undistributed. In an E proposition both the S term and the P term are distributed. In an I proposition both the S term and the P term are undistributed. In an O proposition the S term is undistributed, but the P term is distributed.

The material of this section may be summarized in the following table:

Proposition letter	Quality	Quantity	Terms distributed
A	affirmative	universal	S
E	negative	universal	S and P
I	affirmative	particular	None
O	negative	particular	P

Sample Exercises from Exercise 4.2, Part I

1. No rich men are persons who beg in the street.

   letter name: E
   quantity: universal
   quality: negative
   subject term: rich men (distributed)
   predicate term: persons who beg in the street (distributed)

2. All ducks are birds that waddle.

   letter name: A
   quantity: universal

39

```
quality:          affirmative
subject term:     ducks (distributed)
predicate term:   birds that waddle (undistributed)
```

3. Some medicines are nasty substances.

```
letter name:      I
quantity:         particular
quality:          affirmative
subject term:     medicines (undistributed)
predicate term:   nasty substances (undistributed)
```

4. Some bald people are not persons who wear wigs.

```
letter name:      O
quantity:         particular
quality:          negative
subject term:     bald people (undistributed)
predicate term:   persons who wear wigs (distributed)
```

4.3 THE TRADITIONAL SQUARE OF OPPOSITION

The *traditional square of opposition* is a diagram specifying logical relations among the four types (A, E, I, and O) of categorical propositions, assuming that the S term and the P term do not change from type to type. The square of opposition often allows the truth value of one of the categorical propositions to be determined simply on the basis of the truth value of another of the categorical propositions (with the same subject term and the same predicate term).

Two propositions are *contradictory* if they cannot both be true and cannot both be false. In other words, they must have opposite truth values—it must be the case that exactly one of them is true and the other false. The A and O propositions are contradictory, and the E and I propositions are contradictory.

Two propositions are *contrary* if they cannot both be true but they might both be false. In other words, at least one of them must be false, and possibly both are false. The A and E propositions are contrary.

Two propositions are *subcontrary* if they cannot both be false but they might both be true. In other words, at least one of them must be true, and possibly both are true. The I and O propositions are subcontrary.

A and I propositions are related by *subalternation*. This means that the truth of I may be inferred from the truth of A, according to the traditional square of opposition. The reverse inference, from I to A, however, is invalid. E and O propositions are also related by subalternation: from the truth of E the truth of O may be inferred, but the reverse inference, from the truth of O to the truth of E, is invalid.

It follows from the four relationships presented in the square of opposition that if A is given as true, then E is false, I is true, and O is false. If E is given as true, then A is false, I is false, and O is true. If I is given as true, then E is false, but A and O are undetermined (that is, their truth values cannot be calculated from the information). If O is given as true, then A is false, but E and I are undetermined.

40

It also follows from the traditional square that if A is given as false, then O is true, but E and I are undetermined. If E is given as false, then I is true, but A and O are undetermined. If I is given as false, then A is false, E is true, and O is true. If O is given as false, then A is true, E is false, and I is true.

Sample Exercises from Exercise 4.3, Part I

1. All girls are discontented individuals.

   This proposition is given as true. It is an A proposition. Thus:

   a. "No girls are discontented individuals" is the corresponding E proposition and is false.
   b. "Some girls are discontented individuals" is the corresponding I proposition and is true.
   c. "Some girls are not discontented individuals" is the corresponding O proposition and is false.

2. All girls are discontented individuals.

   This proposition is given as false. Thus:

   a. The corresponding E proposition is undetermined.
   b. The corresponding I proposition is undetermined.
   c. The corresponding O proposition is true.

Additional Exercises for Section 4.3

For each of the following specifications of the S term and the P term, construct the categorical proposition of the indicated type. Tell whether it is true or false. Then, on the basis of this knowledge and nothing else except the logical relations on the traditional square of opposition, tell whether the other three corresponding categorical propositions are true, false, or undetermined.

1. A proposition with S = men and P = mortals.

2. O proposition with S = fish and P = bass.

3. E proposition with S = dogs and P = cats.

4. I proposition with S = chairs and P = antiques.

5. O proposition with S = grasshoppers and P = insects.

6. A proposition with S = numbers and P = even numbers.

7. E proposition with S = authors and P = poets.

8. I proposition with S = horses and P = palominos.

9. E proposition with S = roses and P = plants.

10. O proposition with S = elms and P = trees.

4.4 CONVERSION, OBVERSION, AND CONTRAPOSITION

The operations of conversion, obversion, and contraposition are applied
to categorical propositions to yield new categorical propositions.
Conversion consists of simply switching the subject term with the
predicate term while leaving the quality and the quantity of the proposition unaltered. The result of applying conversion to a categorical
proposition is called the *converse* of the proposition. Thus, for example, the converse of "All dogs are mammals" is "All mammals are dogs."
The converses of E and I propositions are *logically equivalent* to them
(that is, they necessarily have the same truth values). The converses
of A and O propositions are not, in general, logically equivalent to
them.* Similarly, if we form an argument whose premise is a categorical
proposition and whose conclusion is the converse of it, then the argument
is valid if the premise is an E or an I proposition and, in general, is
invalid if the premise is an A or an O proposition. (In the latter case
the argument commits the fallacy of *illicit conversion*.)

Obversion consists of both (1) changing the quality of the proposition (leaving the quantity the same), and (2) negating the predicate
term. To negate the predicate term, one typically attaches the prefix
"non-" to it. The result of obversion is called the *obverse* of the
proposition to which it is applied. The obverse of any categorical
proposition, A, E, I, or O, is logically equivalent to it. Any argument
whose premise is a categorical proposition and whose conclusion is its
obverse is a valid argument.

Contraposition consists of both (1) switching the subject term with
the predicate term (while leaving the quality and quantity of the proposition unaltered), and (2) negating both terms. Thus, for example,
the contrapositive of "All dogs are mammals" is "All non-mammals are
non-dogs." The result of contraposition is called the *contrapositive* of
the proposition to which it is applied. The contrapositives of A propositions and O propositions are logically equivalent to the originals,
while the contrapositives of E and I propositions are not, in general,
logically equivalent to the originals. If we form an argument whose
premise is a categorical proposition and whose conclusion is the contrapositive of it, then the argument is valid if the premise is an A or an
O proposition and, in general, is invalid if the premise is an E or an I
proposition. (In the latter case the argument commits the fallacy of
illicit contraposition.)

Conversion, obversion, and contraposition may be used in sequence to
prove certain arguments valid. There are two basic points to remember.
The first is that doubly negating a term (e.g., non-non-*P*) yields the
equivalent of the term that is doubly negated. The second is that the
operations of conversion and contraposition must be correctly applied:
conversion must be applied only to E and I propositions and contraposition only to A and O propositions. Here is an example of using the operations to show that "All *A* are non-*B*; therefore, no *B* are *A*" is a valid
argument:

> All *A* are non-*B*.
> All non-non-*B* are non-*A*. *contraposition of an* A *proposition*
> All *B* are non-*A*. *replacing "non-non-*B*" by "*B*"*

---

*An exception to this point occurs if the *S* term and the *P* term are
the same, or are synonymous.

42

No *B* are non-non-*A*.   *obversion*

No *B* are *A*.   *replacing "non-non-*A" by "*A"*

Sample Exercises from Exercise 4.4, Part I

1. a. All bores are dreaded creatures.

   Converse: All dreaded creatures are bores.

   These are *not* logically equivalent.

   b. No bankrupts are rich men.

   Converse: No rich men are bankrupts.

   These two *are* logically equivalent.

   c. Some eagles are large birds.

   Converse: Some large birds are eagles.

   These two *are* logically equivalent.

   d. Some bonbons are not chocolate creams.

   Converse: Some chocolate creams are not bonbons.

   These two are *not* logically equivalent.

2. a. All thieves are dishonest individuals.

   Obverse: No thieves are non-dishonest individuals.

      or No thieves are honest individuals.

   These two *are* logically equivalent.

   b. No policemen are persons less than four feet tall.

   Obverse: All policemen are non-(persons less than four feet tall).

   These two *are* logically equivalent.

   c. Some analgesics are inefficient pain relievers.

   Obverse: Some analgesics are not non-(inefficient pain relievers).

   These two *are* logically equivalent.

   d. Some porcupines are not nonswimmers.

   Obverse: Some porcupines are non-nonswimmers.

      or Some porcupines are swimmers.

   These two *are* logically equivalent.

Additional Exercises for Section 4.4

Construct the indicated propositions.

1. The obverse of: Some fish are not bass.

2. The contrapositive of: All angels are principalities.

3. The converse of: All ants are non-butterflies.

4. The obverse of the converse of: No mortals are perfect things.

5. The contrapositive of the obverse of: Some dogs are not cats.

6. The converse of the contrapositive of: No gods are idols.

7. The obverse of the contrapositive of the converse of: All wives are workers.

8. The converse of the contrapositive of the obverse of: No insects are non-spiders.

9. The contrapositive of the obverse of the converse of: Some poets are non-authors.

10. The converse of the obverse of the contrapositive of: Some wolves are not non-females.

4.5 THE MODERN SQUARE OF OPPOSITION
AND THE EXISTENTIAL FALLACY

Problems arise with the traditional square of opposition when it is used in conjunction with categorical statements that make assertions about things that do not exist, that is to say, about terms that have empty denotation. To deal more adequately with such cases we must use the *modern square of opposition*. It is based on an interpretation of universal statements (the A and E propositions) as conditional statements. According to this interpretation, "All S are P" means "If there are any S, then they are P." "No S are P" means "If there are any S, then they are not P." The modern interpretation of the I and O propositions is the same as the traditional interpretation.

The only relation on the traditional square of opposition that is preserved in the modern interpretation is the relation of contradiction. Thus, the modern square of opposition permits fewer inferences than the traditional square. We may use the traditional square of opposition only when we presuppose that the terms in our categorical propositions do not have empty denotation. If we do not want to make this presupposition, we must use the modern square.

The *existential fallacy* is committed in any inference based on the relations of the traditional square of opposition (contradiction excluded) that involves propositions that are not presupposed to make statements only about things that exist. Thus, inferring from "All unicorns are heavy" that "Some unicorns are heavy" commits this fallacy. So, too, does the inference from "All unicorns are heavy" that "It is not the case that no unicorns are heavy."

Sample Exercises from Exercise 4.5

1. All eagles are birds.
   Therefore, some eagles are birds.

44

Since eagles exist, we may use the traditional square of opposition. By subalternation the argument is valid.

2. No mermaids are brunettes.
Therefore, some mermaids are not brunettes.

Since mermaids do not exist, we must use the modern square of opposition. The argument is invalid and commits the existential fallacy.

4.6 VENN DIAGRAMS

Venn diagrams are ways of pictorially representing the informational content of categorical propositions. The basic conventions for such diagrams are as follows.

1. Each term is represented by a circle. (When two terms are involved, the diagram contains two overlapping circles, one for each term.)
2. The area inside the circle for a term represents the extension of that term, and the area outside the circle represents everything not in the extension of that term.
3. The areas of overlap and nonoverlap of the circles represent things in an obvious way, given convention (2). Thus, for example, the football-shaped region of overlap between the two circles represents things that are in both the extensions of the two terms involved.
4. Shading of an area means that the class of things represented by that area is empty; placing an "X" in an area indicates that the correlated class is not empty—that is, that there is at least one thing in it.
5. If a given area is neither shaded out nor filled in with an "X," nothing is said about the corresponding class.

Using Venn diagrams, we may conveniently represent all four of the categorical propositions in their modern interpretations. The A proposition may be represented by

The E proposition may be represented by

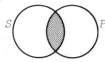

The I proposition may be represented by

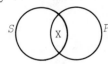

45

The O proposition may be represented by

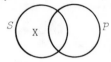

The diagrams show what we noted earlier: that the A and E propositions in their modern interpretations say nothing at all about the existence of anything.

Sample Exercises from Exercise 4.6

1. No debators are prejudiced people.

    Modern interpretation:

2. All pigs are fat animals.

    Modern interpretation:

3. Some newspapers are worthless endeavors.

    Modern interpretation:

4. Some misers are not cheerful individuals.

    Modern interpretation:

4.7 VENN DIAGRAMS: FURTHER APPLICATIONS

Venn diagrams provide a convenient illustration of the inferences involved in the modern square of opposition, as well as of the operations of conversion, obversion, and contraposition. For example, where the A proposition has shading, the O proposition has an "X" and where the E proposition has shading, the I proposition has an "X." This illustrates the contradictory nature of the pair A, O and the pair E, I.

Similarly, if Venn diagrams are constructed for a given categorical proposition and its converse, it is found that the pairs of diagrams match for the E and I propositions but not for the A and O propositions.

This illustrates the valid conversion of E and I propositions and the invalid conversion of the A and O propositions.

If Venn diagrams are constructed for a given categorical proposition and its obverse, it is found that the pair of diagrams match in all four cases. This illustrates the valid obversion of all four of the categorical propositions.

If Venn diagrams are constructed for a given categorical proposition and its contrapositive, it is found that the pairs of diagrams match for the A and O propositions but not for the E and I propositions. This illustrates the valid nature of contraposition for A and O propositions and the invalid nature of contraposition for the E and I propositions.

The text explains the use of Venn diagrams in illustrating inferences involved in the traditional square of opposition.

4.8 TRANSLATING ORDINARY LANGUAGE STATEMENTS INTO CATEGORICAL FORM

Many statements of ordinary life are not, strictly speaking, categorical propositions. Yet their informational content is that of categorical propositions. In order to make such statements amenable to logical analysis after the patterns developed in Chapter 4, it is necessary to translate them into explicit categorical propositions. The following ten rules of thumb facilitate this task. Nevertheless, no set of rules can cover every conceivable case. One must understand the *meaning* of a given statement and then reexpress that meaning, if doing so is possible, as a categorical proposition.

1. The subject and predicate terms of a categorical proposition must be *nouns* or noun substitutes. If a term in a statement is not a noun, it often may be converted into one. For example, adjectives may be nominalized by adding the word "things" to them. Thus, "All pieces of lead are heavy" may be reexpressed as "All pieces of lead are heavy things."

2. The copula of a categorical proposition must be "are" or "are not." If the *verb* in a statement is not of this sort, it may often be converted. For example: "Some dogs run fast" may be reexpressed as "Some dogs are fast runners."

3. Categorical propositions must begin with the quantifiers "no," "some," or "all." If a statement does not start this way, it may often be converted. For instance, *singular propositions* (those about one specific thing) may be reexpressed as universal categorical propositions by using certain *parameters* (phrases like "things identical to," "persons identical to," and so on). Thus, "Socrates is a good philosopher" may be reexpressed as "All persons identical to Socrates are good philosophers." Another example: "This dogwood is now blossoming" may be reexpressed as "All things identical with this dogwood are things that are now blossoming.

4. Statements containing spatial and temporal *adverbs,* such as "everywhere" or "sometimes," may be translated into categorical propositions by employing the words "places" and "times," respectively. Similarly, statements containing *pronouns* like "whoever" or "whatever" may be translated by employing the words "persons" and "things," respectively. For example, "Snow is everywhere" may be reexpressed as "All places are places in which there is snow." "John never goes to school" may be reexpressed as "No times are times when John goes to school."

5. Many statements in ordinary language have implied but *unexpressed quantifiers*. These statements may be translated by making the quantifier explicit. Thus "Donkeys are stubborn" may be reexpressed as "All donkeys are stubborn things." "Children are present" may be reexpressed as "Some children are things that are present."

6. Many statements in ordinary language have *nonstandard quantifiers* that are expressed by words other than the three allowable quantifiers of categorical propositions. In such cases, the statements may often be reexpressed in terms of the three allowable quantifiers. Thus "Several books on this shelf are difficult" may be reexpressed as "Some books on this shelf are books that are difficult to read." In this connection it should be noted that "All *S* are not *P*" is not a standard form categorical proposition. It may be reexpressed, however, either as "No *S* are *P*" or as "Some *S* are not *P*," depending on its meaning. Thus "All that glitters is not gold" may be reexpressed as "Some things that glitter are not things made of gold."

7. Certain *conditional statements* can be reexpressed as categorical propositions. For example, "If a man is tired, then he is hungry" can be reexpressed as "All tired men are hungry men." As in this example, the conditionals that can be translated have the same subject in both the antecedent and the consequent. They always translate as universal categorical propositions. Statements containing "unless" can also often be translated. Thus "Dogs are happy unless they are beaten" becomes "All unbeaten dogs are happy dogs," or "All unhappy dogs are beaten dogs."

8. *Exclusive propositions* (those that involve the words "only" and "none but") may also be translated. Thus "Only dogs are happy animals" becomes "All happy animals are dogs." "None but natural techniques are allowed" becomes "All techniques that are allowed are natural techniques."

9. Statements beginning with "*the only*" are different from those beginning with "only." Usually the words "the only" may simply be replaced with the word "all." Thus "The only flowers I like are roses" is translated as "All flowers that I like are roses."

10. *Exceptive propositions*, like "All except *S* are *P*," must be translated as pairs of conjoined categorical propositions, such as "No *S* are *P*, and all non-*S* are *P*." Exceptive propositions ("all except," "all but") should not be confused with exclusive propositions.

Sample Exercises from Exercise 4.8

1. A prudent man shuns tigers.

   This may be reexpressed as:
   All prudent men are men who shun tigers.

2. Ostriches do not feed on mince pies.

   This may be reexpressed as:
   No ostriches are things that feed on mince pies.

3. No idlers win fame.

   This may be reexpressed as:
   No idlers are persons who win fame.

48

4. Sugar is sweet.

    This may be reexpressed as:
    All things consisting of sugar are sweet things.

Additional Exercises for Section 4.8

Reexpress the following statements as categorical propositions.

1. Only the strong survive.

2. No one not in the club may vote.

3. Wherever you go I will follow.

4. Any tiger is fierce.

5. The only men who will be promoted are sergeants.

6. Only sargeants are men who will be promoted.

7. Elephants are big.

8. All but miscreants will go unpunished.

9. George Washington was the first U.S. president.

10. My father was a carpenter.

11. Men at work. (as on a sign)

12. A whale is a mammal.

13. I will meet you anytime.

14. Dogs are not five-legged.

15. If a man is well-fed, he is content.

16. No one likes broccoli.

17. If you like broccoli, you'll love spinach.

18. A city is prosperous if it has industry.

19. Several people did not like the movie.

20. When you first called, I was surprised.

5
CATEGORICAL
SYLLOGISMS

5.1 STANDARD FORM, MOOD, AND FIGURE

A *syllogism* is a two-premise deductive argument. More specifically, a *categorical syllogism* is an argument in which both the premises and the conclusion are categorical propositions. Furthermore, these three propositions contain a total of three different terms, each used exactly twice, and none is used twice in the same proposition of the argument. In the following discussion, "syllogism" means "categorical syllogism."

The predicate term of the conclusion is called the *major term* of the syllogism. It occurs in only one of the premises, and that premise is called the *major premise* of the syllogism. The subject term of the conclusion is called the *minor term* of the syllogism. It occurs in the premise that does not contain the major term, which is called the *minor premise* of the syllogism. The remaining, or third, term is called the *middle term* of the syllogism. It occurs once in the major premise and once in the minor premise.

A categorical syllogism is in *standard form* if the major premise is listed first, the minor premise second, and the conclusion third. The *mood* of a syllogism in standard form is a list of three letters, where each of these letters is A, E, I, or O. The first letter designates the categorical type of the major premise, the second letter the categorical type of the minor premise, and the third letter the categorical type of the conclusion.

The *figure* of a standard form categorical syllogism is a number from 1 to 4 that designates the *arrangement* of its three terms. Thus, Figure 1 designates the arrangement

$$\frac{...M...P}{...S...M}$$
$$...S...P$$

(Here "S" denotes the minor term, the subject of the conclusion; "P" denotes the major term, the predicate of the conclusion; and "M" denotes the middle term.)

Figure 2 designates the arrangement

$$\frac{...P...M}{...S...M}$$
$$...S...P$$

Figure 3 designates the arrangement

$$...M...P$$
$$\underline{...M...S}$$
$$...S...P$$

Figure 4 designates the arrangement

$$...P...M$$
$$\underline{...M...S}$$
$$...S...P$$

The mood and figure of a categorical syllogism can be determined by putting its major premise first, its minor premise second, and its conclusion third, and then noting both the types of its propositions and the arrangement of its terms.

Moreover, a mood and figure designation, such as AII-2, can be fleshed out by simply drawing the form of the indicated figure (in this case, Figure 2), and then writing in the quantifiers and copulas to make each of the propositions match the indicated mood (in this case, AII). Thus, AII-2 can be fleshed out as

All P are M.
Some S are M.
Some S are P.

Each such fleshed-out syllogism represents a logical form of an actual syllogism. Assuming that there are no semantic connections among the terms of the syllogism, a syllogism is valid if and only if its form is valid. In the modern interpretation of categorical propositions, exactly fifteen of the mood and figure designations represent valid forms:

Figure 1: AAA, EAE, AII, EIO
Figure 2: EAE, AEE, EIO, AOO
Figure 3: IAI, AII, OAO, EIO
Figure 4: AEE, IAI, EIO

In the traditional interpretation of categorical propositions, certain other forms are also valid.

Sample Exercises from Exercise 5.1, Part I

1. No sailors are romantic individuals, so no sailors are poets, since all poets are romantic individuals.

P = poets
S = sailors
R = romantic individuals

In standard form this argument is:

All P are R.
No S are R.
No S are P.

This argument is AEE-2. It is valid.
51

2. Some lions are not coffee drinkers, for some fierce creatures are lions and no coffee drinkers are fierce creatures.

C = coffee drinkers
L = lions
F = fierce creatures

In standard form this argument is:

> No C are F.
> Some F are L.
> Some L are not C.

This argument is EIO-4. It is valid.

Sample Exercises from Exercise 5.1, Part II

1. OAE-3
   Fleshed out, this is: Some M are not P.
   All M are S.
   No S are P.

2. EIA-4
   Fleshed out, this is: No P are M.
   Some M are S.
   All S are P.

Additional Exercises for Section 5.1

I. Flesh out the following mood and figure designations. Determine whether the resultant syllogism is valid (according to the modern interpretation of categorical propositions) by checking the mood and figure designation against the list of valid syllogisms.

1. AII-2	6. EAE-2
2. AAA-3	7. AOI-4
3. EIO-4	8. EEO-3
4. IEA-1	9. EOO-1
5. OOO-2	10. EAE-4

II. Identify the major term (P), the minor term (S), and the middle term (M) of the following syllogisms. Place them into standard form (if they are not already in standard form). Identify their mood and figure. By checking the list of valid syllogisms, determine whether they are valid or invalid (according to the modern interpretation of categorical propositions).

1. No men are islands.
   All islands are continents.
   Some continents are not men.

52

2. No islands are men.
    Some islands are continents.
    Some continents are not men.

3. Some seals are walruses.
    No walruses are tigers.
    Some tigers are not seals.

4. All elephants are pachyderms.
    Some pachyderms are not large animals.
    Some elephants are not large animals.

5. No dogs are cats.
    All cats are felines.
    No dogs are felines.

6. Some dogs are cockers.
    All cockers are spaniels.
    Some spaniels are not dogs.

7. Some horses are stallions, for some horses are roans, and all
    roans are stallions.

8. No ants are insects. So no grasshoppers are insects, since
    all ants are grasshoppers.

9. Since all figurines are art objects, some art objects are
    not paintings, for no paintings are figurines.

10. No drivers are racers, since all racers are speeders and no
    speeders are drivers.

5.2 VENN DIAGRAMS

Venn diagrams provide a convenient technique for testing the validity of
categorical syllogisms. In using Venn diagrams in conjunction with
categorical syllogisms, the general conventions specified in Section 4.6
prevail, except that we now have three terms and three circles.
    To use a Venn diagram to test for the validity of a categorical
syllogism, follow this procedure:

1. Enter the information of the premises into the diagram. (Do
not enter the conclusion.)
2. Look at the resulting diagram to see whether it implies the
information of the conclusion. If it does, the syllogism is valid. If
it does not, the syllogism is invalid.

Several pointers will facilitate using this procedure:

1. Diagram universal premises before particular premises.
2. When diagramming a premise, concentrate only on the two circles
representing the terms of that premise. The third circle can usually be
ignored.
3. When placing an "X" in the diagram, note that it always goes
into an area that is split by the third (largely ignored) circle. This

third circle divides that area into two parts. If neither of these parts has been shaded, the "X" is placed on the line from the third circle that divides the two parts. If one of these parts has been shaded, the "X" is placed in the unshaded part. (Note: It will never happen that both the parts have been shaded.)

Sample Exercises from Exercise 5.2, Part I

1. All conceited children are greedy brats.
    Some greedy brats are Girl Scouts.
    Therefore, some Girl Scouts are conceited children.

    The form of this argument is AII-4. Its Venn diagram is:

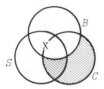

    This argument is invalid both from the modern and traditional view-points.

2. No students anxious to learn are failures.
    Some students anxious to learn are romantics.
    Therefore, some romantics are not failures.

    The form of this argument is EIO-3. Its Venn diagram is:

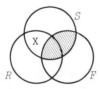

    This argument is valid both from the modern and traditional view-points.

Sample Exercises from Exercise 5.2, Part II

1. No P are M.
    All S are M.

    The Venn diagram for these two premises is:

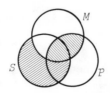

54

From the diagram it may be seen that the conclusion "No S are P" may validly be drawn.

2. Some M are S.
   Some P are not M.

The Venn diagram for these two premises is:

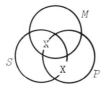

From the diagram it may be seen that no conclusion may validly be drawn.

Additional Exercises for Section 5.2

Construct Venn diagrams for the twenty examples in "Additional Exercises for Section 5.1, Parts I and II" and use them to determine whether the syllogisms are valid or invalid. Check your answers against the list of valid syllogisms (according to the modern interpretation of the categorical propositions).

5.3 RULES AND FALLACIES

Valid syllogisms conform to certain rules, and these rules may accordingly be used as crosschecks to the Venn diagram test for validity. Following are five rules. When one of these rules is broken, a corresponding formal fallacy is committed. The first two rules have to do with the distribution of terms, and the last three have to do with the quality and quantity of the propositions in the syllogisms.
   In using Rules 1 and 2, recall that

       In the **A** proposition, S is distributed, P is undistributed.
       In the **E** proposition, S and P are both distributed.
       In the **I** proposition, S and P are both undistributed.
       In the **0** proposition, S is undistributed, P is distributed.

    Rule 1: The middle term must be distributed in at least one of the premises.

    Fallacy: If this rule is broken, the fallacy committed is *undistributed middle.*

    Example: All P are M.
                 <u>All S are M.</u>
                 All S are P.   Here M is undistributed in both premises.

    Rule 2: If a term is distributed in the conclusion, it must be distributed in the premise.

Fallacy: If this rule is broken, the fallacy committed is either *illicit major* (if P is distributed in the conclusion but undistributed in the major premise) or *illicit minor* (if S is distributed in the conclusion but undistributed in the minor premise).

Example: All M are P.
All S are M.
No S are P. Here P is distributed in the conclusion but undistributed in the major premise. (illicit major)

Example: All P are M.
All M are S.
No S are P. Here S is distributed in the conclusion but undistributed in the minor premise. (illicit minor)

Rule 3: Two negative premises are not allowed.

Fallacy: If this rule is broken, the fallacy committed is *exclusive premises.*

Example: No P are M.
No S are M.
No S are P. Here both premises are negative.

Rule 4: One negative premise is allowed if and only if the conclusion is negative.

Fallacy: If this rule is broken, the fallacy committed is either *drawing a negative conclusion from affirmative premises* or *drawing an affirmative conclusion from a negative premise.*

Example: All P are M.
All S are M.
No S are P. Here a negative conclusion is drawn from affirmative premises.

Example: No P are M.
Some S are M.
Some S are P. Here an affirmative conclusion is drawn from a negative premise.

Rule 5: If both premises are universal, the conclusion cannot be particular.

Fallacy: If this rule is broken, the *existential fallacy* is committed.

Example: All P are M.
All S are M.
Some S are P.

Note: Rule 5 applies only to the modern interpretation of the categorical propositions.

56

Sample Exercises from Exercise 5.3

1. **AAA-3**

    Fleshed out, this becomes:

    All *M* are *P*.
    All *M* are *S*.
    ───────────
    All *S* are *P*.

    Since *S* is distributed in the conclusion but not in the minor
    premise, this syllogism commits the fallacy of illicit minor.

2. **IAI-2**

    Fleshed out, this becomes:

    Some *P* are *M*.
    All *S* are *M*.
    ───────────
    Some *S* are *P*.

    Since *M* is undistributed in both premises, this syllogism commits
    the fallacy of undistributed middle.

3. **EIO-1**

    Fleshed out, this becomes:

    No *M* are *P*.
    Some *S* are *M*.
    ───────────
    Some *S* are not *P*.

    This syllogism commits none of the fallacies and is accordingly
    valid.

4. **AAI-2**

    Fleshed out, this becomes:

    All *P* are *M*.
    All *S* are *M*.
    ───────────
    Some *S* are *P*.

    Since a particular conclusion is drawn from two universal premises,
    this syllogism commits the existential fallacy. Since *M* is undis-
    tributed in both premises, it also commits the fallacy of undistrib-
    uted middle.

Additional Exercises for Section 5.3

Flesh out the following figure and mood designations and test the result
for validity using the five rules.

1. **AAA-4**   3. **EII-2**

2. **AAA-1**   4. **EEE-3**

5. AII-3   8. AEA-3

6. OAO-4   9. AEE-1

7. IEA-1   10. IAI-3

5.4 REDUCING THE NUMBER OF TERMS

Many two-premise arguments contain negated terms, so that the number of terms in the entire argument exceeds three. Thus, these arguments are not categorical syllogisms in the strict sense. Nevertheless, through use of the operations of conversion, obversion, and contraposition, such arguments can often be replaced by logically equivalent arguments that *are* categorical syllogisms in the strict sense.

The important thing to remember in employing these operations is that conversion may be applied only to E and I propositions and that contraposition may be applied only to A and O propositions.

> *Example:* All non-*P* are non-*M*.
> All non-*M* are non-*S*.
> No *S* are non-*P*.

Applying contraposition to both premises and obversion to the conclusion, we may replace this argument with the logically equivalent argument

> All *M* are *P*.
> All *S* are *M*.
> All *S* are *P*.

This syllogism is, of course, of the form AAA-1 and is valid. Consequently, the original argument is valid.

Sample Exercise from Exercise 5.4

1. Some intelligible statements are true statements, because all unintelligible statements are meaningless statements and some false statements are meaningful statements.

    Let *I* = intelligible statements, *T* = true statements, and *M* = meaningful statements. Then, ordering premises and conclusion, the argument becomes:

    > Some non-*T* are *M*.
    > All non-*I* are non-*M*.
    > Some *I* are *T*.

    By applying conversion and then obversion to the first premise, and contraposition to the second premise, we obtain:

    > Some *M* are not *T*.
    > All *M* are *I*.
    > Some *I* are *T*.

58

This is the syllogism OAI-3. It commits the fallacy of drawing an affirmative conclusion from a negative premise.

Additional Exercises for Section 5.4

By rearranging propositions and applying the operations of conversion, obversion, and contraposition, make these arguments into standard form categorical syllogisms. Identify whether they are valid or invalid.

1. No one is crazy and some financiers are not non-persons. So some financiers are sane.

2. All valid arguments are intelligible ones. So some chains of reasoning are not valid arguments, since some chains of reasoning are intelligible arguments.

3. Some happy persons are not solvent, since some bankers are insolvent and no bankers are happy persons.

4. All snacks are fattening foods and all fattening foods are non-nutritious. So all nutritious foods are non-snacks.

5. Some scholars are not felons. The reason for this is that no felons are innocent and some scholars are not guilty.

5.5 ORDINARY LANGUAGE ARGUMENTS

Many two-premise arguments in ordinary language do not look much like standard form categorical syllogisms. However, by a judicious process of translation, some of them may be converted into standard form categorical syllogisms and then tested for validity using the techniques presented in the chapter. Perhaps the best way to see this is to consider the solved exercises from the text.

Sample Exercises from Exercise 5.5

1. Only good students can pass this exam. Since Theresa passed it, it follows that she's a good student.

   This argument may be reexpressed as:

   All students who pass this exam are good students.
   All students identical to Theresa are students who pass
   this exam.
   _____
   All students identical to Theresa are good students.

   This is the syllogism AAA-1 and is valid.

2. It must have rained lately because the streets are wet, and the streets are always wet after it rains.

   This argument may be reexpressed as:

All times soon after it rains are times when the
streets are wet.
All times identical to the present are times when
the streets are wet.
All times identical to the present are times soon
after it rains.

This is the syllogism AAA-2. Since it commits the fallacy of
undistributed middle, it is invalid.

Additional Exercises for Section 5.5

Reexpress the following arguments as standard form categorical syllogisms, and test them for validity using the five rules for valid
syllogisms.

1. I like all drinks and this is a drink, so I like it.

2. If you go to town, you buy a dress. Since you went to town today,
    you must have bought a dress today.

3. Nothing immoral is fattening, and overeating is fattening. It
    follows that overeating is not immoral.

4. Wherever you go I will follow, but I won't follow you to Bali.
    So you won't go to Bali.

5. If you have any money, we will spend it. Some of your money is
    ill-gotten gains. So we will spend some ill-gotten gains.

5.6   ENTHYMEMES

An *enthymeme* is an argument that is expressible as a categorical syllogism but that is missing either a premise or the conclusion. To evaluate
an enthymeme, supply the missing premise or conclusion, express the
syllogism in standard form, and apply the usual tests for validity.

Sample Exercises from Exercise 5.6

1. All of my students are intelligent, so George can't be one of my
    students.

    This enthymeme is missing the premise: George is not intelligent.

2. Only geraniums grow in the east garden, and those flowers on the
    table were picked there this morning.

    This enthymeme is missing the conclusion: Those flowers on the
    table are geraniums.

A *sorites* is a sequence of categorical syllogisms in which the intermediate conclusions have been omitted. A sorites is in standard form when each of the component propositions is a standard form categorical proposition, when the predicate term of the conclusion is in the first premise, when each term occurs exactly twice, and when each premise after the first has a term in common with the preceding one. To evaluate a sorites, express it in standard form, supply the intermediate conclusions, and then break the sorites up into its separate component categorical syllogisms; then test each of the syllogisms for validity. The sorites is valid if each component is valid. Otherwise, it is invalid.

Sample Exercises from Exercise 5.7

1.   No *B* are *C*.
     Some *D* are *C*.
     All *A* are *B*.
     Some *D* are not *A*.

In standard form this sorites becomes:

     All *A* are *B*.
     No *B* are *C*.
     Some *D* are *C*.
     Some *D* are not *A*.

The intermediate conclusion (supposed to follow from the first two premises) is: No *A* are *C*.

Thus, the sorites breaks up into two syllogisms:

     All *A* are *B*.   No *A* are *C*.
     No *B* are *C*.   and   Some *D* are *C*.
     No *A* are *C*.   Some *D* are not *A*.

The Venn diagrams for these two syllogisms are:

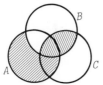 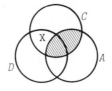

Both are valid. Consequently, the sorites itself is valid.

2. No C are D.
    All A are B.
    Some C are not B.
    Some D are not A.

In standard form this sorites becomes:

> All A are B.
> Some C are not B.
> No C are D.
> Some D are not A.

The intermediate conclusion is: Some C are not A.

Thus, the sorites breaks up into two syllogisms:

All A are B.   Some C are not A.
Some C are not B. and No C are D.
Some C are not A.   Some D are not A.

The Venn diagrams for these two syllogisms are:

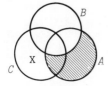 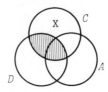

The first of these is valid, but the second is invalid. Thus, the sorites as a whole is invalid.

6

PROPOSITIONAL LOGIC

6.1 SYMBOLS AND TRANSLATION

As we have seen, a great deal of logic involves the search for valid argument forms. In *propositional logic* this quest continues. Here, however, the forms we are concerned with have as their fundamental elements symbols denoting entire statements or propositions. We may define a *simple* (*atomic*) statement as one containing no other statement as a part; and a *compound* (*molecular*) statement is one that contains at least two statements. Upper case letters are used to denote atomic statements.

Propositional logic also relies on special symbols denoting *connectives*—that is, words or groups of words that have the function of combining one or two propositions into a single larger proposition:

Connective	Name	Meaning
~	negation	not; it is not the case that
•	conjunction	and
v	disjunction	or
⊃	conditional	if...then; only if
≡	biconditional	if and only if

Note: The conjunction sign also stands for words like "but," "however," "and also," and so forth. The disjunction sign stands for the *inclusive* "or," sometimes written as "and/or." The conditional sign is also used for phrases like "given that," "on the condition that," and so forth. The meaning of the biconditional is that the propositions flanking it are the same in truth value—that is, both true or both false. (See the text for further explanations of the meanings of the five basic connectives.)

If we let A and B be two propositions, the various relationships between A and B may be symbolized, using the five basic connectives. Some of the most important symbolizations are:

Combination	Translation
A is true.	A
A is false.	$\sim A$
A isn't so.	$\sim A$

63

Combination	Translation
Either A or B (or both).	$A \vee B$
A unless B.	$A \vee B$*
A or else B.	$A \vee B$
If A, then B.	$A \supset B$
A if B.	$B \supset A$
A only if B.	$A \supset B$
Only if A, B.	$B \supset A$
A if and only if B.	$A \equiv B$
A is a necessary condition for B.	$B \supset A$
A is a sufficient condition for B.	$A \supset B$
A necessary condition for A is B.	$A \supset B$
A sufficient condition for A is B.	$B \supset A$
A necessary and sufficient condition for A is B.	$A \equiv B$
A is a necessary and sufficient condition for B.	$A \equiv B$
Neither A nor B.	$\sim(A \vee B)$
Either not A or not B.	$\sim A \vee \sim B$
Neither not A nor not B.	$\sim(\sim A \vee \sim B)$
Both not A and not B.	$\sim A \cdot \sim B$
Not both A and B.	$\sim(A \cdot B)$

The connectives allow us to combine not only atomic propositions with one another but also an atomic proposition with a molecular one and molecular propositions with each other. When combining molecular propositions into larger molecular propositions, care must be taken to insert parentheses so that the combination is unambiguous. For example, the proposition $A \supset B \supset C$ is ambiguous: it may mean either $A \supset (B \supset C)$ or $(A \supset B) \supset C$, and these two propositions are not logically equivalent.

Sample Exercises from Exercise 6.1

1. It is not the case that Austria embargoes steel imports.

   Translation: $\sim A$

2. Austria embargoes steel imports and Belgium does not develop nuclear weapons.

   Translation: $A \cdot \sim B$

3. Either Canada curtails grain exports or Denmark decreases military spending.

   Translation: $C \vee D$

4. Both Austria and Belgium embargo steel imports.

   Translation: $A \cdot B$

---

* A unless B may also be used in an "exclusive" sense, to be translated as "$A \equiv \sim B$."

Additional Exercises for Section 6.1

Translate the following into symbolizations of propositional logic, using the upper case letters A = Al goes to town, B = Betty goes to town, C = Cathy goes to town.

1. Al and Betty do not both go to town.

2. Al and Betty both do not go to town.

3. Either Al or Cathy does not go to town, but Betty does go.

4. Neither Al nor Betty goes to town.

5. If Al or Betty goes to town, Cathy does not go.

6. Al goes to town only if Betty goes but Cathy doesn't.

7. Al does not go to town if and only if both Betty and Cathy do.

8. A necessary condition of Al's not going to town is Betty's and Cathy's both not going.

9. A necessary and sufficient condition for Al's going to town is Betty's and Cathy's not both going.

10. If Al goes to town, then Betty goes to town if Cathy doesn't.

6.2 TRUTH FUNCTIONS

If the truth value of a molecular proposition is entirely determined by the truth values of its atomic components (independent of the specific meaning of these atomic components), then the molecular proposition is said to be a *truth function* of its components. All molecular propositions built up out of atomic propositions by means of the five connectives so far introduced are truth functions. Another way of expressing this fact is to say that the five connectives are themselves *truth functional connectives*.

We can express the truth functionality of the five connectives by showing in a list or table exactly how the connectives render the truth value of a molecular proposition computable from the truth values of its components. In order to do so, we need to introduce the idea of a *statement variable*: a variable that can represent any statement or proposition. Statement variables are represented by lower case letters, such as "p" and "q." When statement variables are combined by means of connectives, we have *statement forms*. For example, "p," "$p \vee q$," and "$p \cdot q$" are statement forms. When we substitute any propositions uniformly for the statement variables in a statement form, a statement is produced. Such a statement is called a *substitution instance* of the statement form.

With the notions of statement variable and statement form, we can now express the truth functionality of the connectives. For instance, consider negation. We may express its truth functionality thusly:

p	$\sim p$
T	F
F	T

65

This table means that, regardless of what proposition is used to replace "p," if it is true, then its negation is false (regardless of its meaning), and if it is false, then its negation is true (again regardless of its meaning).

The table for conjunction is as follows:

p	q	$p \cdot q$
T	T	T
T	F	F
F	T	F
F	F	F

The meaning of this table is that a conjunction of any two propositions is true only when both the left-hand conjunct and the right-hand conjunct are true (regardless of the meanings of these conjuncts).
The tables for other connectives are:

p	q	$p \vee q$
T	T	T
T	F	T
F	T	T
F	F	F

p	q	$p \supset q$
T	T	T
T	F	F
F	T	T
F	F	T

p	q	$p \equiv q$
T	T	T
T	F	F
F	T	F
F	F	T

These tables are in effect rules for calculating the truth value of any molecular proposition built up from atomic propositions by means of the five connectives, provided that we are given truth values for the atomic propositions themselves. For instance, suppose A is the proposition "2 and 2 make 4," B is the proposition "Reagan is President (in 1982)," and C is the proposition "Austin is the capital of California." Then the truth value of $(A \vee B) \supset C$; that is, of "If either 2 and 2 make 4 or Reagan is President (in 1982), then Austin is the capital of California" can be computed to be false. For $A \vee B$ can be computed to be true from the table for disjunction (first row, where the left-hand disjunct and the right-hand disjunct are both true), and then the entire proposition's truth value can be computed from the table for the conditional (second row, where the left-hand member, the antecedent, is true and the right-hand member, the consequent, is false). The calculation may also be expressed as follows:

In performing such calculations, the important thing to remember is to work from inside out, from simpler to more complex.

Sample Exercises from Exercise 6.2, Part II

1. It is not the case that Hitler ran the Third Reich.

    This has the form $\sim H$. Since it is true that Hitler ran the Third Reich, the resulting proposition is false.

2. Nixon resigned the Presidency and Lincoln wrote the Gettysburg Address.

This has the form $N \cdot L$. Since it is true that Nixon resigned the Presidency and true that Lincoln wrote the Gettysburg Address, the resulting proposition is true.

3. Caesar governed China or Lindbergh crossed the Atlantic.

This has the form $C \vee L$. Since it is false that Caesar governed China and true that Lindbergh crossed the Atlantic, the resulting proposition is true.

4. Hitler ran the Third Reich and Nixon did not resign the Presidency.

This has the form $H \cdot \sim N$. Since it is true that Hitler ran the Third Reich, and false that Nixon did not resign the Presidency, the resulting proposition is false.

Additional Exercises for Section 6.2

Compute the truth values of the following propositions. Assume that A, B, and C are true propositions and that X, Y, and Z are false propositions.

1. $A \supset (B \supset X)$

2. $\sim A \vee [X \supset (\sim X)]$

3. $(A \equiv X) \equiv (B \equiv Y)$

4. $(A \equiv Z) \equiv (X \equiv Y)$

5. $X \supset \sim(X \supset \sim X)$

6. $(A \vee X) \supset (Y \vee Z)$

7. $[(A \cdot B) \cdot C] \equiv [A \cdot (X \vee Y)]$

8. $[(\sim A) \equiv (\sim X)] \vee (Y \vee C)$

9. $[(X \supset Y) \supset \sim Y] \supset \sim X$

10. $[X \supset (\sim X \supset Y)] \supset [(Y \supset \sim Z) \supset X]$

6.3 TRUTH TABLES FOR PROPOSITIONS

In the previous section it was shown how a truth value could be calculated for any molecular proposition built up from the five connectives, given a particular set of truth values for its atomic constituents. Obviously, a truth value could be calculated for such a molecular proposition given *any* truth value assignment for its atomic constituents. The notion of a truth table for a proposition is the notion of a table in which, for *every* truth value assignment to the atomic constituents of a proposition, a truth value is calculated and expressed. For any n letters, there are 2^n possible truth assignments to these letters taken together. Thus, the truth table for a proposition composed of n atomic constituents will have 2^n rows in it, one row for each truth assignment. For example, here is the truth table for $P \vee \sim Q$:

$$
\begin{array}{c|c|cc}
P & \vee & \sim & Q \\
\hline
T & T & F & T \\
T & T & T & F \\
F & F & F & T \\
F & T & T & F \\
\end{array}
$$

In the column representing the proposition as a whole, we may find all true's, or we may find all false's, or we may find a mixture (at least one true and at least one false). In the first event, the proposition is called a *logical truth* or a *tautology*; in the second case, it is called a *logical falsehood* or a *self-contradiction*; and in the third case, it is called a *contingency*.

Two propositions having the same letters as constituents are said to be *logically equivalent* if they have exactly the same columns in their truth tables. A little reflection will show that two propositions are logically equivalent only if the proposition obtained by combining them with the material equivalence sign ($\equiv$) is itself a tautology. Two propositions are logically *contradictory* if their columns are exactly the opposite (a T for every F and vice versa). A little reflection will show that two propositions are logically contradictory only when the proposition obtained by combining them with the material equivalence sign is a self-contradiction.

Sample Exercises from Exercise 6.3, Part I

1. $A \supset (A \supset A)$

$$
\begin{array}{c|c|ccc}
T & T & T & T & T \\
F & T & F & T & F \\
\end{array}
$$

The proposition is tautologous.

2. $(D \supset D) \supset D$

$$
\begin{array}{ccc|c|c}
T & T & T & T & T \\
F & T & F & F & F \\
\end{array}
$$

The proposition is contingent.

Sample Exercises from Exercise 6.3, Part II

1. $\sim D \vee T$ $\sim (D \cdot \sim T)$

$$
\begin{array}{cc|c|c}
F & T & T & T \\
F & T & F & F \\
T & F & T & T \\
T & F & T & F \\
\end{array}
\qquad
\begin{array}{c|cccc}
T & T & F & F & T \\
F & T & T & T & F \\
T & F & F & F & T \\
T & F & F & T & F \\
\end{array}
$$

The propositions are logically equivalent.

68

2.　　~K ⊃ L　　　　K ⊃ ~L

F T	T	T		T	F	F T
F T	T	F		T	T	T F
T F	T	T		F	T	F T
T F	F	F		F	T	T F

The propositions are neither logically equivalent nor logically contradictory.

Additional Exercises for Section 6.3

I.　By constructing truth tables, determine whether the following propositions are contradictions, tautologies, or contingencies.

1.　$P \lor {\sim}P$

2.　$P \supset {\sim}P$

3.　$P \cdot {\sim}P$

4.　$P \lor Q$

5.　$(P \lor Q) \supset P$

6.　$(P \cdot Q) \supset P$

7.　$P \supset (Q \supset P)$

8.　$[(P \lor Q) \cdot {\sim}P] \cdot {\sim}Q$

9.　$[P \cdot (Q \supset P)] \equiv [Q \cdot (Q \supset P)]$

10.　$[P \equiv (Q \equiv P)] \equiv [Q \equiv (P \equiv Q)]$

II.　By constructing truth tables, determine which of the following pairs are logically equivalent propositions.

1.　P　　　　　　　　$P \supset {\sim}P$

2.　P　　　　　　　　${\sim}P \supset P$

3.　$P \lor Q$　　　　　${\sim}P \lor {\sim}Q$

4.　$P \supset Q$　　　　${\sim}P \lor Q$

5.　$P \equiv (Q \equiv P)$　　Q

6.4　ARGUMENT FORMS AND FALLACIES

Many arguments in propositional logic are substitution instances of argument forms that have specific names and are valid (in the sense that any substitution instance of them is valid). Six such valid forms will be discussed in this section. Some arguments in propositional logic have invalid forms with specific names. With an invalid form, substitution instances are not, in general, valid arguments. Several such invalid forms will be discussed here.

Valid Forms

Disjunctive syllogism (DS)　　　$p \lor q$
　　　　　　　　　　　　　　　$\underline{{\sim}p}$
　　　　　　　　　　　　　　　　q

69

Hypothetical syllogism (HS)

$$p \supset q$$
$$\underline{q \supset r}$$
$$p \supset r$$

Modus ponens (MP)

$$p \supset q$$
$$\underline{p}$$
$$q$$

Modus tollens (MT)

$$p \supset q$$
$$\underline{\sim q}$$
$$\sim p$$

Constructive dilemma (CD)

$$(p \supset q) \cdot (r \supset s)$$
$$\underline{p \lor r}$$
$$q \lor s$$

Destructive dilemma (DD)

$$(p \supset q) \cdot (r \supset s)$$
$$\underline{\sim q \lor \sim s}$$
$$\sim p \lor \sim r$$

Invalid Forms

Fallacy of affirming the consequent (AC)

$$p \supset q$$
$$\underline{q}$$
$$p$$

Fallacy of denying the antecedent (DA)

$$p \supset q$$
$$\underline{\sim p}$$
$$\sim q$$

Notice that the invalid form affirming the consequent is easily confused with *modus ponens*. Similarly, the invalid form denying the antecedent is easily confused with *modus tollens*. Another invalid form, nameless but easily confused with the disjunctive syllogism, is:

$$p \lor q$$
$$\underline{p}$$
$$q$$

Sample Exercises from Exercise 6.4, Part I

1. $N \supset C$
   $\underline{\sim C}$
   $\sim N$ This argument is *modus tollens*

2. $S \supset F$
   $\underline{F \supset \sim L}$
   $S \supset \sim L$ This argument is hypothetical syllogism

3. $A \lor \sim Z$
   $\underline{\sim Z}$
   A This is an invalid argument form

4. $(S \supset \sim P) \cdot (\sim S \supset D)$
   $\underline{S \lor \sim S}$
   $\sim P \lor D$ This argument is constructive dilemma

Additional Exercises for Section 6.4

Identify the forms of the following valid arguments.

1. If Al goes to town, then so will Betty. Al goes to town. So, then, will Betty.

2. If Al goes to town, then so will Betty. Betty will not go to town. So Al does not go to town.

3. Either Al goes to town or Betty stays home. Al does not go to town. So Betty stays home.

4. If Al goes to town, then Betty stays home. But if Betty stays home, then supper will not be purchased. So if Al goes to town, supper will not be purchased.

5. If Al goes to town, then Betty stays home. But if Al does not go to town, then Cathy stays home. Since Al either goes or doesn't go to town, either Betty stays home or Cathy stays home.

6. If Al plays in the tournament, then Betty will win it, and if Kenny plays in the tournament, then Cathy will win it. Either Betty will not win the tournament or Cathy will not win it. So either Al will not play in it or Kenny will not play in it.

7. If no one likes fish in this town, then this store will soon be bankrupt. But no one does like fish in this town. The conclusion is inevitable that this store will soon be bankrupt.

8. If John came home last night on time, his mother is happy today. His mother is not happy today. Therefore, John did not come home last night on time.

9. Either you go to class or I go to class. But you don't go. So I go.

10. If I represent myself in court, then I have a fool for a lawyer. But if I have a fool for a lawyer, then I have a fool for a client. So if I represent myself in court then I have a fool for a client.

6.5   TRUTH TABLES FOR ARGUMENTS

Just as truth tables may be constructed for single propositions, so, too, may truth tables be constructed for arguments (which are, after all, collections of propositions). To do so, we must represent all the propositions of the argument in a single table. That is, a column must be made for each proposition in the argument. If the argument is in English, it must be symbolized first, letting capital letters stand for each atomic proposition in the argument. For example, the argument "If John is happy, then Sam is happy; John is happy; therefore, Sam is happy" may be represented by:

$$J \supset S$$
$$\frac{J}{S}$$

71

Its truth table may be represented by:

```
J ⊃ S  /  J  //  S
T T T     T      T
T F F     T      F
F T T     F      T
F T F     F      F
```

A truth table may be used to test an argument for validity in the following way. If there is a row in the table in which every premise is true and the conclusion is false, the argument is invalid. If there is no such row, the argument is valid. For example, the truth table above shows that the argument is valid—there is no row in which all the premises are true and the conclusion is false.

Notice that any argument with a tautological conclusion is valid and that any argument with self-contradictory premises (premises such that there is no row in the truth table in which all of them are true) is also valid.

Sample Exercises from Exercise 6.5, Part I

1. If Annie gets the pretzels, then Bob buys the beer. Therefore, if Annie does not get the pretzels, then Bob does not buy the beer.

   Translation: $A \supset B$ // $\sim A \supset \sim B$

   ```
   A ⊃ B      ~A ⊃ ~B
   T T T      F T T F T
   T F F      F T T T F
   F T T      T F F F T
   F T F      T F T T F
   ```

   In the third row, the premise is true and the conclusion is false. So the argument is invalid.

2. Charles gets the chips. Therefore, either Charles gets the chips or Denise brings the dip.

   Translation: C // $C \lor D$

   ```
   C       C ∨ D
   T       T T T
   T       T T F
   F       F T T
   F       F F F
   ```

   There is no row in which the premise is true and the conclusion is false, so the argument is valid.

Additional Exercises for Section 6.5

Test the following symbolized arguments for validity using truth tables.

1. $P \lor Q$ / $P \supset \sim P$ // Q 3. $P \lor Q$ // $P \cdot Q$

2. $P \supset Q$ / $\sim P \supset P$ // Q 4. $P \cdot Q$ // $P \equiv Q$

72

5. $P \cdot \sim Q$ $//$ $P \equiv Q$ 8. $\sim P \vee Q$ $/$ $\sim Q \vee R$ $//$ $Q \equiv P$

6. $P \supset Q$ $/$ $Q \supset R$ $//$ $R \supset P$ 9. P $/$ Q $//$ $R \vee \sim R$

7. $\sim(P \equiv Q)$ $/$ $\sim Q$ $//$ P 10. $P \vee Q$ $/$ $P \supset \sim P$ $/$ $\sim Q$ $//$ R

6.6   INDIRECT TRUTH TABLES FOR ARGUMENTS

The indirect truth table technique—also known as the shorter truth
table technique—for testing for the validity of arguments is usually
a faster method of testing for validity than constructing an entire truth
table. It is based on the fact that an argument is invalid if and only
if there is at least one row in its truth table where all the premises
are true and the conclusion false. Instead of constructing the entire
table, we may attempt to construct a row in which the premises are true
and the conclusion false. If we succeed in doing so, the argument is
invalid. If we are unsuccessful—if the assumption that there is a row
in which all premises are true and the conclusion is false leads to a
contradictory truth assignment to one or more letters—then the argument
is valid.

To apply the indirect technique, we must try to find a truth assignment to the letters of an argument for which the premises are true and
the conclusion false. If our attempt is successful, the argument is
shown to be invalid. If our attempt leads to a contradictory assignment
to one or more letters, the argument is valid.

Example: Consider the valid argument $P \supset Q$ $/$ P $//$ Q. This is
an instance of *modus ponens* and is valid. If we try to make premises
true and conclusion false, we must at least make Q (the conclusion)
false and P (the second premise) true. But with P true and Q false, the
first premise, $P \supset Q$, cannot be made true. This method shows the argument to be valid.

Example: Consider the invalid argument $P \supset Q$ $/$ Q $//$ P. Here
we must make P (the conclusion) false and Q (the second premise) true.
Now $P \supset Q$ becomes true and we have invented a truth assignment that makes
all the premises true and the conclusion false. This method shows the
argument to be invalid.

Sample Exercises from Exercise 6.6

1. $\underline{B \equiv C}$
    $\sim C \supset \sim B$

    The only way to make the conclusion false is to make C false and
    B true. Doing this, however, makes the premise false, so there is
    no assignment that makes the premise true and the conclusion false.
    This shows the argument to be valid.

2. $\sim E \vee F$
    $\underline{\sim E}$
    $\sim F$

    The only way to make the conclusion false is to make F true. The
    only way to make the second premise true is to make E false. With
    F true and E false, the first premise becomes true, so we have an

73

assignment making premises true and conclusion false. Thus, the argument is invalid.

3. $\dfrac{\sim(I \equiv J)}{\sim(I \supset J)}$

This example is a little more complex than the two preceding ones. There are *two* ways to make the premise true, namely with I true and J false or with I false and J true. If I is true and J is false, then the conclusion is true, so this assignment does not lead to a demonstration that the argument is invalid. But with I false and J true, the conclusion becomes false. This, therefore, is an assignment making the premise true and the conclusion false; it accordingly shows the argument to be invalid.

4. $\dfrac{P \supset (Q \supset R)}{(P \cdot Q) \supset R}$

The only way to make the conclusion false is with P true, Q true, and R false. But this makes the premise false. So the argument is valid.

Additional Exercises for Section 6.6

Determine whether the following arguments are valid or invalid, using the indirect truth table technique.

1. $P \supset Q$
    $\dfrac{P \cdot R}{Q \cdot R}$

2. $\dfrac{P \vee Q}{\sim Q \supset \sim P}$

3. $\dfrac{P \supset Q}{P \supset (P \cdot Q)}$

4. $P \supset \sim P$
    $\dfrac{P \vee Q}{Q}$

5. $P \supset Q$
    $\dfrac{\sim Q \supset Q}{\sim P \supset P}$

6. $P \supset Q$
    $\dfrac{Q \supset \sim Q}{P \supset \sim P}$

7. $P \equiv Q$
    $\dfrac{Q}{P}$

8. P
    $\dfrac{Q}{P \equiv Q}$

9. P
    $\dfrac{\sim Q}{P \equiv Q}$

10. $\dfrac{P \vee Q}{P \equiv Q}$

74

7

NATURAL DEDUCTION IN PROPOSITIONAL LOGIC

7.1 RULES OF IMPLICATION I

Every substitution instance of a valid argument form is valid. This fact is the key to understanding *natural deduction*, a method of demonstrating the validity of arguments in propositional logic. In natural deduction, certain valid argument forms (and eventually certain forms of logical equivalences) are used as *rules* for deducing a proposition from one or more others. For example, since $p \supset q$ / p // q is a valid argument form, then from, say, $A \supset B$ and A, B can be validly deduced. A *proof* or *derivation* of an argument is a sequence of propositions that lead from the premises of the argument to its conclusion in the following way: each proposition in the sequence is either itself one of the premises of the argument or else can be deduced from one or more *previous* members of the sequence by means of one of the rules of deduction. It can be shown in detail—and it is more or less intuitively clear—that any argument for which a proof exists is a valid argument.

As a matter of fact, any valid argument form (or any logically equivalent form) can be used as a rule of deduction. For the purpose of simplicity, most systems of natural deduction employ only a small number of forms as *rules of inference*. In this text there are eighteen such rules. The first four are

1. $p \supset q$
   $\underline{p\qquad}$ *modus ponens* (MP)
   q

2. $p \supset q$
   $\underline{\sim q\qquad}$ *modus tollens* (MT)
   $\sim p$

3. $p \supset q$
   $\underline{q \supset r}$ hypothetical syllogism (HS)
   $p \supset r$

4. $p \vee q$
   $\underline{\sim p\qquad}$ disjunctive syllogism (DS)
   q

The basic task in mastering natural deduction is to learn to construct proofs. This task is not always simple and straightforward. The text gives a number of rules of thumb for constructing derivations,

75

but there is no substitute for practice. In some ways natural deduction is like the game of chess; in order to play it well, one must first learn the permitted moves by heart and then, with practice, acquire a "feel" for the strategy of the activity.

Sample Exercises from Exercise 7.1, Part II

(1) 1. $(G \equiv J) \lor (B \supset P)$
     2. $\sim (G \equiv J)$ / $B \quad P$
     3. $B \supset P$ 1,2; DS

(2) 1. $(K \cdot O) \supset (N \lor T)$
     2. $K \cdot O$ / $N \lor T$
     3. $N \lor T$ 1,2; MP

(3) 1. $(M \lor P) \supset \sim K$
     2. $D \supset (M \lor P)$ / $D \supset \sim K$
     3. $D \supset \sim K$ 1,2; HS

(4) 1. $\sim \sim (R \lor W)$
     2. $S \supset \sim (R \lor W)$ / $\sim S$
     3. $\sim S$ 1,2; MT

(5) 1. $\sim C \supset (A \supset C)$
     2. $\sim C$ / $\sim A$
     3. $A \supset C$ 1,2; MP
     4. $\sim A$ 2,3; MT

(6) 1. $F \lor (D \supset T)$
     2. $\sim F$
     3. D / T
     4. $D \supset T$ 1, 2, DS
     5. T 3, 4, MP

(7) 1. $(K \cdot B) \lor (L \supset E)$
     2. $\sim(K \cdot B)$
     3. $\sim E$ / $\sim L$
     4. $L \supset E$ 1, 2, DS
     5. $\sim L$ 3, 4, MT

(8) 1. $P \supset (G \supset T)$
     2. $Q \supset (T \supset E)$
     3. P
     4. Q / $G \supset E$
     5. $G \supset T$ 1, 3, MP
     6. $T \supset E$ 2, 4, MP
     7. $G \supset E$ 5, 6, HS

(9) 1. $\sim W \supset [\sim W \supset (X \supset W)]$
     2. $\sim W$ / $\sim X$
     3. $\sim W \supset (X \supset W)$ 1, 2, MP
     4. $X \supset W$ 2, 3, MP
     5. $\sim X$ 2, 4, MT

Additional Exercises for Section 7.1

Using the first four rules of inference, construct proofs of the
following arguments.

(1) 1. $X \supset (Y \supset Z)$
    2. X
    3. Y / Z

(2) 1. $X \lor (Y \lor Z)$
    2. $\sim X$
    3. $\sim Y$ / Z

(3) 1. $X \lor \sim Y$
    2. $\sim X$
    3. $Z \supset Y$ / $\sim Z$

(4) 1. $X \supset (Y \lor Z)$
    2. $W \supset X$
    3. W
    4. $\sim Y$ / Z

(5) 1. $X \supset (\sim Y \supset \sim Z)$
    2. $\sim Y$
    3. $Y \lor X$ / $\sim Z$

(6) 1. $X \supset Y$
    2. $Y \supset Z$
    3. $\sim Z$ / $\sim X$

(7) 1. $X \supset (Y \supset Z)$
    2. $X \supset (Z \supset W)$
    3. $T \lor X$
    4. $\sim T$ / $Y \supset W$

(8) 1. $X \lor (Y \cdot Z)$
    2. $(Y \cdot Z) \supset W$
    3. $X \supset T$
    4. $\sim T$ / W

(9) 1. $\sim X \lor \sim Y$
    2. $\sim X \supset Z$
    3. $\sim Z$
    4. $Y \lor W$ / W

(10) 1. $X \supset (X \supset \sim Y)$
     2. $Y \lor \sim T$
     3. X
     4. $W \supset T$ / $\sim W$

7.2   RULES OF IMPLICATION II

In this section four additional rules of derivation are presented.
As with the first four, they are valid argument forms.

5. $(p \supset q) \cdot (r \supset s)$
   $\underline{p \lor r \hspace{3cm}}$ constructive dilemma (CD)
   $q \lor s$

6. $\underline{p \cdot q}$ simplification (Simp)
   p

7. p
   $\underline{q \hspace{1cm}}$ conjunction (Conj)
   $p \cdot q$

8. $\underline{p \hspace{1cm}}$ addition (Add)
   $p \lor q$

These rules may be used in connection with the first four rules. The
first eight rules have the common characteristic that they must be
applied to *whole lines* in proofs, and not merely to parts of lines.
Without this restriction, the erroneous deduction

77

$$\frac{(p \cdot q) \supset r}{p \supset r}$$

might be thought to be justified by simplification, just to take one example. (The rules introduced later in this chapter, called rules of replacement, are not covered by this restriction.)

Sample Exercises from Exercise 7.2, Part II

(1) 1. $\sim M \supset Q$
    2. $R \supset \sim T$
    3. $\sim M \vee R$ / $Q \vee \sim T$
    4. $(\sim M \supset Q) \cdot (R \supset \sim T)$ 1, 2, Conj
    5. $Q \vee \sim T$ 3, 4, CD

(2) 1. $E \supset (A \cdot C)$
    2. $A \supset (F \cdot E)$
    3. E / F
    4. $A \cdot C$ 1, 3, MP
    5. A 4, Simp
    6. $F \cdot E$ 2, 5, MP
    7. F 6, Simp

(3) 1. $G \supset (S \cdot T)$
    2. $(S \vee T) \supset J$
    3. G / J
    4. $S \cdot T$ 1, 3, MP
    5. S 4, Simp
    6. $S \vee T$ 5, Add
    7. J 2, 6, MP

(4) 1. $(L \vee T) \supset (B \cdot G)$
    2. $L \cdot (K \equiv R)$ / $L \cdot B$
    3. L 2, Simp
    4. $L \vee T$ 3, Add
    5. $B \cdot G$ 1, 4, MP
    6. B 5, Simp
    7. $L \cdot B$ 3, 6, Conj

Additional Exercises for Section 7.2

Use the first eight rules of inference to construct proofs for the following arguments.

(1) 1. $(X \vee Y) \supset Z$
    2. $(Z \vee T) \supset W$
    3. X / W

(2) 1. $X \supset (Y \cdot Z)$
    2. $Y \supset K$
    3. W
    4. $W \supset X$ / K

(3) 1. $X \supset (Y \vee Z)$
    2. $Y \supset W$
    3. $Z \supset K$
    4. X / $W \vee K$

(4) 1. $X \supset Y$
    2. $(\sim X \vee W) \supset K$
    3. $\sim Y \cdot Z$ / $K \vee T$

(5) 1. $X \vee (Y \vee Z)$
    2. $\sim Y \cdot W$
    3. $\sim X \cdot T$ / $Z \vee T$

(6) 1. $(X \supset Y) \cdot (Z \supset W)$
    2. $(K \cdot L) \cdot M$
    3. $K \supset (X \vee Z)$ / $Y \vee W$

(7) 1. $(X \supset Y) \cdot L$
    2. $(Y \supset Z) \cdot M$
    3. $(X \supset Z) \supset [(X \supset Y) \supset W]$ / W

(8) 1. $(X \cdot Y) \vee (Z \cdot W)$
    2. $(X \cdot Y) \supset L$
    3. $\sim L \cdot M$
    4. $Z \supset (N \cdot O)$ / N

(9) 1. $(X \supset Y) \cdot Z$
    2. $X \cdot L$
    3. $(X \supset Y) \supset M$
    4. $(Y \cdot M) \supset (Z \cdot K)$ / $Z \vee W$

(10) 1. $X \supset P$
     2. $X \cdot R$
     3. $P \supset (Q \cdot S)$
     4. $(P \cdot Q) \supset (P \equiv Q)$ / $P \equiv Q$

(11) 1. $A \supset (B \supset C)$
     2. $A \cdot X$
     3. $B \cdot (Y \cdot Z)$ / $C \cdot A$

(12) 1. $(B \supset C) \supset A$
     2. $A \supset X$
     3. $\sim X \cdot Y$
     4. $D \supset (B \supset C)$ / $\sim A \cdot \sim D$

(13) 1. $(A \supset B) \cdot (C \supset D)$
     2. $(B \supset E) \cdot (F \supset G)$
     3. $(A \supset E) \supset (H \cdot I)$
     4. $H \supset J$ / $H \cdot J$

(14) 1. $(A \cdot B) \supset (C \vee D)$
     2. $C \supset E$
     3. $A \supset B$
     4. $A \cdot F$
     5. $(D \supset G) \cdot H$ / $(A \cdot B) \cdot (E \vee G)$

(15) 1. $A \supset B$
      2. $C \vee A$
      3. $C \supset D$
      4. $\sim D$ $/ (B \cdot \sim C) \vee E$

7.3 RULES OF REPLACEMENT I

We saw in Sections 7.1 and 7.2 how valid argument forms may be used as rules of inference in natural deduction. Forms of logical equivalences may also be used as rules of inference. Every substitution instance of a form of logical equivalence is a logical equivalence; moreover, either one of a pair of logically equivalent expressions may be substituted for the other in a proof without loss of validity.

Five forms of logical equivalence are given in this section:

9. $\sim(p \cdot q)$ is logically equivalent to $(\sim p \vee \sim q)$.
   $\sim(p \vee q)$ is logically equivalent to $(\sim p \cdot \sim q)$.

These two statements are known as DeMorgan's Rule (DM).

10. $(p \vee q)$ is logically equivalent to $(q \vee p)$.
    $(p \cdot q)$ is logically equivalent to $(q \cdot p)$.

These two rules are known as commutativity (Com).

11. $[p \vee (q \vee r)]$ is logically equivalent to $[(p \vee q) \vee r]$.
    $[p \cdot (q \cdot r)]$ is logically equivalent to $[(p \cdot q) \cdot r]$.

These two rules are known as associativity (Assoc).

12. $[p \cdot (q \vee r)]$ is logically equivalent to $[(p \cdot q) \vee (p \cdot r)]$.
    $[p \vee (q \cdot r)]$ is logically equivalent to $[(p \vee q) \cdot (p \vee r)]$.

These two rules are known as Distribution (Dist).

13. p is logically equivalent to $\sim\sim p$.

This is known as double negation (DN).

These and the remaining rules of replacement may be applied not only to whole lines in proofs—as the rules of implication must be—but to parts of lines as well. Thus, going from

$$(p \cdot q) \supset r$$

to

$$(q \cdot p) \supset r$$

by the rule of commutativity is quite proper.

Sample Exercises from Exercise 7.3, Part II

(1) 1. $(\sim M \supset P) \cdot (\sim N \supset Q)$
    2. $\sim(M \cdot N)$ / $P \vee Q$
    3. $\sim M \vee \sim N$ 2, DM
    4. $P \vee Q$ 1, 3, CD

(2) 1. $J \vee (K \cdot L)$
    2. $\sim K$ / J
    3. $\sim K \vee \sim L$ 2, Add
    4. $\sim(K \cdot L)$ 3, DM
    5. $(K \cdot L) \vee J$ 1, Com
    6. J 4, 5, DS

(3) 1. $R \supset \sim B$
    2. $D \vee R$
    3. B / D
    4. $\sim\sim B$ 3, DN
    5. $\sim R$ 1, 4, MT
    6. $R \vee D$ 2, Com
    7. D 5, 6, DS

(4) 1. $(O \vee M) \supset S$
    2. $\sim S$ / $\sim M$
    3. $\sim(O \vee M)$ 1, 2, MT
    4. $\sim O \cdot \sim M$ 3, DM
    5. $\sim M \cdot \sim O$ 4, Com
    6. $\sim M$ 5, Simp

Additional Exercises for Section 7.3

(1) 1. $\sim(X \cdot Y)$
    2. X
    3. $Y \vee Z$ / Z

(2) 1. $X \cdot (Y \vee Z)$
    2. $\sim(X \cdot Y)$
    3. $(Z \cdot X) \supset K$ / K

(3) 1. $\sim X \vee Y$
    2. $\sim Y \vee Z$
    3. $X \cdot W$ / $(X \cdot Y) \cdot Z$

(4) 1. $(X \vee Y) \supset Z$
    2. $\sim(Z \vee W)$ / $\sim Y$

(5) 1. $X \cdot (Y \cdot Z)$
    2. $(Y \cdot X) \supset (W \cdot T)$
    3. $(T \cdot Z) \supset L$ / $(Y \cdot W) \cdot Z$

(6) 1. $\sim X \supset T$
    2. $W \cdot \sim T$
    3. $(X \vee Y) \supset Z$ / $W \cdot Z$

(7) 1. $\sim X$
    2. $\sim(X \cdot Y) \supset \sim W$ / $\sim(W \cdot Z)$

(8) 1. $\sim(X \lor \sim X)$ / Y

(9) 1. X
    2. $(\sim Y \lor X) \supset Z$
    3. $\sim(X \cdot Z) \lor W$ / $(W \cdot X) \cdot Z$

(10) 1. $X \cdot \sim Z$
    2. $(Y \lor X) \supset \sim W$ / $\sim(Z \lor W)$

7.4 RULES OF REPLACEMENT II

The remaining five rules of replacement are:

14. $(p \supset q)$ is logically equivalent to $(\sim q \supset \sim p)$.

This rule is called transposition (Trans).

15. $(p \supset q)$ is logically equivalent to $(\sim p \lor q)$.

This rule is called material implication (Impl).

16. $(p \equiv q)$ is logically equivalent to $[(p \supset q) \cdot (q \supset p)]$.
$(p \equiv q)$ is logically equivalent to $[(p \cdot q) \lor (\sim p \cdot \sim q)]$.

These two rules together are known as material equivalence (Equiv).

17. $[(p \cdot q) \supset r]$ is logically equivalent to $[p \supset (q \supset r)]$.

This rule is known as exportation (Exp).

18. p is logically equivalent to $(p \lor p)$.
p is logically equivalent to $(p \cdot p)$.

These two rules are known as tautology (Taut).

Remember that all the rules of replacement may be applied to parts of lines as well as to whole lines.

Sample Exercises from Exercise 7.4, Part II

(1) 1. $(J \cdot R) \supset H$
    2. $(R \supset H) \supset M$
    3. $\sim(P \lor \sim J)$ / $M \cdot \sim P$
    4. $J \supset (R \supset H)$ 1, Exp
    5. $\sim P \cdot \sim\sim J$ 3, DM
    6. $\sim\sim J \cdot \sim P$ 5, Com
    7. $\sim\sim J$ 6, Simp
    8. J 7, DN
    9. $R \supset H$ 4, 8, MP
   10. M 2, 9, MP
   11. $\sim P$ 5, Simp
   12. $M \cdot \sim P$ 10, 11, Conj

(2) 1. $(B \supset G) \cdot (F \supset N)$
    2. $\sim(G \cdot N)$ $/ \sim(B \cdot F)$
    3. $\sim G \vee \sim N$ 2, DM
    4. $(\sim G \supset \sim B) \cdot (F \supset N)$ 1, Trans
    5. $(\sim G \supset \sim B) \cdot (\sim N \supset \sim F)$ 4, Trans
    6. $\sim B \vee \sim F$ 3, 5, CD
    7. $\sim(B \cdot F)$ 6, DM

(3) 1. T $/ S \supset T$
    2. $T \vee \sim S$ 1, Add
    3. $\sim S \vee T$ 2, Com
    4. $S \supset T$ 3, Impl

(4) 1. $\sim(U \cdot W) \supset X$
    2. $U \supset \sim U$ $/ \sim(U \vee \sim X)$
    3. $\sim U \vee \sim U$ 2, Impl
    4. $\sim U$ 3, Taut
    5. $\sim U \vee \sim W$ 4, Add
    6. $\sim(U \cdot W)$ 5, DM
    7. X 1, 6, MP
    8. $\sim\sim X$ 7, DN
    9. $\sim U \cdot \sim\sim X$ 4, 8, Conj
   10. $\sim(U \vee \sim X)$ 9, DM

Additional Exercises for Section 7.4

(1) 1. X
    2. $(Y \supset X) \supset Z$ $/ X \cdot Z$

(2) 1. $X \supset Y$
    2. $(Y \vee \sim X) \supset (Y \supset Z)$ $/ \sim Z \supset \sim X$

(3) 1. X
    2. Y $/ X \equiv Y$

(4) 1. X
    2. $X \supset \sim Y$ $/ X \equiv \sim Y$

(5) 1. $X \supset Y$
    2. $X \supset Z$ $/ X \supset (Y \cdot Z)$

(6) 1. $X \supset (Y \cdot Z)$ $/ (X \supset Y) \cdot (X \supset Z)$

(7) 1. $X \supset Z$
    2. $Y \supset Z$ $/ (X \vee Y) \supset Z$

(8) 1. $(X \vee Y) \supset Z$ $/ (X \supset Z) \cdot (Y \supset Z)$

(9) 1. $X \supset (X \cdot Y)$
    2. $[(X \cdot Y) \vee (\sim X \cdot Y)] \supset Y$ $/ Y \supset Y$

(10) 1. $(X \cdot Y) \supset X$
    2. Y
    3. $(X \supset X) \supset X$ $/ X \cdot Y$

(11) 1. $A \supset (B \lor C)$
     2. $\sim B$ $/ \ A \supset C$

(12) 1. $A \supset (B \lor C)$
     2. $B \supset C$ $/ \ A \supset C$

(13) 1. $(A \supset B) \supset (B \supset A)$ $/ \ B \supset A$

(14) 1. A
     2. $\sim B$ $/ \sim (A \equiv B)$

(15) 1. $\sim (A \equiv B)$
     2. A $/ \sim B$

7.5 CONDITIONAL PROOF

Our system of eighteen rules, although powerful, is still not complete; that is, there are valid arguments for which our rules do not permit the construction of a proof. Two examples of such valid arguments are

$$X \ // \ Y \lor \sim Y$$

and

$$X \supset Y \ // \ X \supset (X \cdot Y)$$

With the addition of *conditional proof* to our system, however, the rules become complete: a proof may be constructed for any valid argument of propositional logic.

The fundamental idea of conditional proof may be viewed as an analog or extension of the rule of exportation. Recall that according to this rule $p \supset (q \supset r)$ is logically equivalent to $(p \cdot q) \supset r$. Analogously, it is a fact that an argument

$$p \ // \ q \supset r$$

is valid if and only if the argument

$$p \ / \ q \ // \ r$$

is valid. More generally, for any number of premises p_1, p_2, ..., p_n the argument

$$p_1 \ / \ p_2 \ / \ ... \ / \ p_n \ // \ q \supset r$$

is valid if and only if the argument

$$p_1 \ / \ p_2 \ / \ ... \ / \ p_n \ / \ q \ // \ r$$

is valid. This implies that to prove an argument with a conditional conclusion $q \supset r$ valid, it is sufficient to assume the antecedent q of that conditional and then from this assumption, together with the premises of the argument, deduce the consequent r of that conditional. The process of carrying out this sort of deduction is called conditional proof (CP).

84

Conditional proof may be diagrammatically represented in this way:

```
 ─
 ─
 ─
 ─
        q          CP
        ─
        ─
        ─
        r
   q ⊃ r           CP
```

In this diagram, q is the assumption. (Any proposition may be assumed in this way at any time.) The indented lines (called the *scope* of the assumption) all follow from the premises only conditionally (that is, with the help of the assumption). At the nonindented line $q ⊃ r$, the assumption is said to be *discharged*. That is, $q ⊃ r$ follows unconditionally from the original premises alone. (An assumption may be discharged at any time, provided that the diagrammatic format is followed.)

Sample Exercises from Exercise 7.5, Part I

(1)
1. $N ⊃ O$
2. $N ⊃ P$ / $N ⊃ (O \cdot P)$
3. N CP
4. O 1, 3, MP
5. P 2, 3, MP
6. $O \cdot P$ 4, 5, Conj
7. $N ⊃ (O \cdot P)$ 3–6, CP

(2)
1. $F ⊃ E$
2. $(F \cdot E) ⊃ R$ / $F ⊃ R$
3. F CP
4. E 1, 3, MP
5. $F \cdot E$ 3, 4, Conj
6. R 2, 5, MP
7. $F ⊃ R$ 3–6, CP

(3)
1. $G ⊃ T$
2. $(T \lor S) ⊃ K$ / $G ⊃ K$
3. G CP
4. T 1, 3, MP
5. $T \lor S$ 4, Add
6. K 2, 5, MP
7. $G ⊃ K$ 3–6, CP

(4)
1. $(G \lor H) ⊃ (S \cdot T)$
2. $(T \lor U) ⊃ (C \cdot D)$ / $G ⊃ C$
3. G CP
4. $G \lor H$ 3, Add
5. $S \cdot T$ 1, 4, MP
6. $T \cdot S$ 5, Com
7. T 6, Simp
8. $I \lor U$ 7, Add
9. $C \cdot D$ 2, 8, MP
10. C 9, Simp
3. $G ⊃ C$ 3–10, CP

Additional Exercises for Section 7.5

Use CP in proving the following arguments valid.

(1)
1. $(X \lor Y) ⊃ (Z \cdot W)$ / $Y ⊃ W$

(2)
1. $(X \lor Y) ⊃ [(Z \lor W) ⊃ R]$ / $(X \cdot W) ⊃ R$

(3)
1. $X ⊃ Y$
2. $Z ⊃ W$ / $(X \lor Z) ⊃ (Y \lor W)$

(4)
1. $X ⊃ Y$
2. $Z ⊃ W$ / $(X \cdot Z) ⊃ (Y \cdot W)$

(5) 1. $(X \lor Y) \supset [(Z \lor W) \supset R]$ $/ \ X \supset (Z \supset R)$

(6) 1. $X \supset Y$
    2. $Z \supset W$ $/ \ (\sim Y \cdot \sim W) \supset (\sim X \cdot \sim Z)$

(7) 1. $X \supset (Y \cdot Z)$
    2. $Z \supset (X \cdot W)$ $/ \ X \equiv Z$

(8) 1. $(X \lor Y) \supset Z$
    2. $(\sim X \lor \sim L) \supset (\sim Z \cdot \sim W)$ $/ \ X \equiv Z$

(9) 1. $X \supset Y$
    2. $Z \supset Y$ $/ \ (X \lor Z) \supset Y$

(10) 1. $\sim(X \cdot Y)$
     2. $\sim[Z \cdot (Y \lor W)]$ $/ \ Y \supset (\sim X \cdot \sim Z)$

7.6 INDIRECT PROOF

Indirect proof, or proof by *reductio ad absurdum*, is a technique familiar to many students of plane geometry. It consists in assuming the opposite of what is to be proved and then deriving a contradiction from this assumption and the other premises. When a contradiction is shown, it may be concluded that what was originally to be proved has been proved.

    Indirect proof may be represented as a special application of conditional proof in the following way. Suppose some conclusion q is to be proved from some premises; suppose also that by assuming the opposite of q (that is, $\sim q$), a contradiction (for example, $r \cdot \sim r$) can be deduced. We may represent this situation as follows:

$$
\begin{array}{ll}
- & \\
- & \\
- & / \ q \\
\sim q & \text{CP} \\
- & \\
- & \\
- & \\
r \cdot \sim r &
\end{array}
$$

We may continue deducing as follows:

$$
\begin{array}{ll}
r & \text{Simp} \\
\sim r \cdot r & \text{Com} \\
\sim r & \text{Simp} \\
r \lor q & \text{Add} \\
q & \text{DS} \\
\sim q \supset q & \text{CP} \\
\sim \sim q \lor q & \text{Impl} \\
q \lor q & \text{DN} \\
q & \text{Taut}
\end{array}
$$

This representation shows that an indirect proof is in effect a conditional proof of a particular sort, in which deduction is carried out right on through the contradiction. It would be unnecessarily repetitive to insist that every time this technique is employed the steps of the deduction that follow the contradiction should be explicitly listed. Accordingly, we may employ the following format for indirect proof (IP):

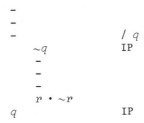

A slightly different but obviously equivalent format for indirect proof is:

```
    -
    -
    -                        / ~q
          q                  IP
          -
          -
          -
          r • ~r
  ~q                         IP
```

In employing these formats, we can use *any* proposition in the place of *r*.

Sample Exercises from Exercise 7.6, Part I

(1) 1. $(S \lor T) \supset \sim S$ $/ \sim S$
    2. $\sim \sim S$ IP
    3. S 2, DN
    4. $S \lor T$ 3, Add
    5. $\sim S$ 1, 4, MP
    6. $S \cdot \sim S$ 3, 5, Conj
    7. $\sim S$ 2-6, IP

    or:

    2. S IP
    3. $S \lor T$ 2, Add
    4. $\sim S$ 1, 3, MP
    5. $S \cdot \sim S$ 2, 4, Conj
    6. $\sim S$ 2-5, IP

(2) 1. $(K \supset K) \supset R$
    2. $(R \lor M) \supset N$ $/ N$
    3. $\sim N$ IP
    4. $\sim (R \lor M)$ 2, 3, MT
    5. $\sim R \cdot \sim M$ 4, DM
    6. $\sim R$ 5, Simp
    7. $\sim (K \supset K)$ 1, 6, MT
    8. $\sim (\sim K \lor K)$ 7, Impl
    9. $\sim \sim K \cdot \sim K$ 8, Dist
    10. $K \cdot \sim K$ DN
    11. N 3-10, IP

Additional Exercises for Section 7.6

Use IP in proving the following arguments valid.

(1) 1. X / $Y \lor \sim Y$

(2) 1. $X \cdot Y$
    2. $Y \supset Z$ / $Z \lor W$

(3) 1. $X \supset Y$
    2. $Y \supset \sim Y$ / $\sim X$

(4) 1. $\sim X \supset X$
    2. $X \supset Y$
    3. $\sim Y \lor Z$ / Z

(5) 1. $X \supset Y$
    2. $Z \supset W$
    3. $\sim Y \lor T$
    4. $\sim U \supset \sim W$
    5. $\sim X \supset Z$ / $T \lor U$

7.7 PROVING LOGICAL TRUTHS

The techniques of conditional proof and indirect proof furnish a new
technique for showing that certain propositions are logical truths—that
is, tautologies.

A proposition of the form $p \supset q$ is a tautology if and only if the
argument p / q is a valid argument. Thus, in order to show that $p \supset q$
is a tautology, it is sufficient to assume p and then to derive q validly
from p. This process may be represented in the format of CP in an
obvious way:

$$p \qquad \text{CP}$$
$$-$$
$$-$$
$$-$$
$$q$$
$$p \supset q \qquad \text{CP}$$

Moreover, a proposition p is a tautology if and only if $\sim p$ is a
self-contradiction, and any proposition is a self-contradiction if and
only if an explicit contradiction—a proposition of the form $q \cdot \sim q$—may
be derived validly from it. Thus, in order to show p to be a tautology,
it is sufficient to assume p and to derive an explicit contradiction
from it. This process may be represented in the format of IP as follows:

$$\sim p \qquad \text{IP}$$
$$-$$
$$-$$
$$-$$
$$q \cdot \sim q$$
$$p \qquad \text{IP}$$

In effect, then, a proposition may be shown tautologous by deriving it from no premises at all, by means of CP or IP. In such a derivation it is convenient to represent the proposition that is to be shown tautologous as the conclusion of an argument having no premises.

Sample Exercises from Exercise 7.7

(1) / $P \supset [(P \supset Q) \supset Q]$

1.	P	CP
2.	$P \supset Q$	CP
3.	Q	1, 2, MP
4.	$(P \supset Q) \supset Q$	2, 3, CP
5.	$P \supset [(P \supset Q) \supset Q]$	1-4, CP

(2) / $(\sim P \supset Q) \lor (P \supset R)$

1.	$\sim[(\sim P \supset Q) \lor (P \supset R)]$	IP
2.	$\sim(\sim P \supset Q) \cdot \sim(P \supset R)$	1, DM
3.	$\sim(\sim\sim P \lor Q) \cdot \sim(P \supset R)$	2, Impl
4.	$\sim(\sim\sim P \lor Q)$	3, Simp
5.	$\sim(P \lor Q)$	4, DN
6.	$\sim P \cdot \sim Q$	5, DM
7.	$\sim P$	6, Simp
8.	$\sim(P \supset R) \cdot \sim(\sim\sim P \lor Q)$	3, Com
9.	$\sim(P \supset R)$	8, Simp
10.	$\sim(\sim P \lor R)$	9, Impl
11.	$\sim\sim P \cdot \sim R$	10, DM
12.	$\sim\sim P$	11, Simp
13.	P	12, DN
14.	$P \cdot \sim P$	7, 13, Conj
15.	$(\sim P \supset Q) \lor (P \supset R)$	1, 14, IP

Additional Exercises for Section 7.7

Use CP or IP to show the following propositions to be tautologies.

(1) $P \supset [P \cdot (Q \lor \sim Q)]$

(2) $P \supset [\sim P \supset (P \lor P)]$

(3) $[(P \supset Q) \supset P] \supset P$

(4) $(P \supset Q) \lor (P \cdot \sim Q)$

(5) $(P \lor Q) \lor [\sim P \cdot (Q \supset \sim Q)]$

8
PREDICATE LOGIC

8.1 SYMBOLS AND TRANSLATION

In *predicate logic* the fundamental component of representation of propositions is the *predicate*. We shall use upper case letters to stand for predicates. Thus, the letter A might stand for the predicate of being altruistic. With this symbolization, the proposition "Socrates is altruistic" could be represented as "A(Socrates)." If we use a lower case letter s to stand for Socrates and omit the really unnecessary parentheses, the same proposition can be represented as As. If a lower case p is used to stand for Plato, then the proposition "Plato is altruistic" can be represented by Ap. In general, we shall allocate the lower case letters of the alphabet—with the exception of x, y, and z—as symbols to stand for individuals; they are called *individual constants*.

These conventions of predicate logic can be combined with those of propositional logic in a straightforward way. Thus, the proposition "If Socrates is altruistic, then Plato is altruistic" can be represented as $As \supset Ap$; the proposition "Socrates is altruistic but Plato is not" can be represented as $As \cdot {\sim}Ap$, and so on.

Representing quantified propositions in predicate logic requires a little more symbolic apparatus. First, we require the idea of an *individual variable*. We shall allocate the lower case letters x, y, and z for use as individual variables. Such variables, which are similar to the variables used in algebra, may be thought of as *ranging over* absolutely all individuals—as referring indifferently to anything at all. Individual variables figure into symbolizations in two ways: they are part of *logical quantifiers*, and they are attached to predicates just as individual constants are attached to predicates. There are two logical quantifiers, the universal quantifier and the existential quantifier. The *universal quantifier*, written (x) and read "for any x," is used to express a universal logical quantification. For example, $(x)Ax$ says that for any x, x is altruistic or, in other words, that everything is altruistic. The *existential quantifier*, written $(\exists x)$ and read as "there exists an x such that," is used to express a particular logical quantification. For example, $(\exists x)Ax$ says that there exists an x such that x is altruistic or, in other words, that something (at least one thing) is altruistic. The existential quantifier may also be read as "for some x." Accordingly, $(\exists x)Ax$ may also be read as "for some x, x is altruistic.

More generally, the universal and existential quantifiers can be attached to any significant context containing variables. Thus, $(x)(Ax \vee {\sim}Ax)$ means that everything is either altruistic or not

90

altruistic. This fact means that we can, for example, symbolize the four standard types of categorical propositions with the apparatus of predicate logic. The A proposition, "All S are P," means (in the modern interpretation) "If anything is an S then it is a P." In other words, it means "For any x, if x is an S then x is a P." Thus, the A proposition may be symbolized as:

$$(x)(Sx \supset Px)$$

Similarly, the E proposition may be symbolized:

$$(x)(Sx \supset \sim Px)$$

The I proposition becomes:

$$(\exists x)(Sx \cdot Px)$$

The O proposition becomes:

$$(\exists x)(Sx \cdot \sim Px)$$

With the apparatus of predicate logic, a great many quantified propositions can be expressed. The text contains many examples of this usage of predicate logic.

Sample Exercises from Exercise 8.1

6. If Gertrude is correct, then the Taj Mahal is made of marble.

Letting g stand for Gertrude and t for the Taj Mahal, we get:

$$Cg \supset Mt$$

7. Gertrude is not correct only if the Taj Mahal is made of granite.

$$\sim Cg \supset Gt$$

8. A thoroughbred is a horse.

$$(x)(Tx \supset Hx)$$

9. A thoroughbred won the race.

$$(\exists x)(Tx \cdot Wx)$$

Additional Exercises for Section 8.1

Translate the following statements into the symbolism of predicate logic, using the indicated letters as predicates.

1. Snakes are reptiles. (S, R)

2. If a snake is a rattler, then it is poisonous. (S, R, P)

3. If a snake is poisonous, then it is either a rattler or a cobra. (S, P, R, C)

4. Only poisonous snakes are rattlers. (*P*, *S*, *R*)

5. Some poisonous snakes are rattlers. (*P*, *S*, *R*)

6. A rattler is poisonous only if it is a snake. (*R*, *P*, *S*)

7. A cobra is a rattler if and only if it is not poisonous. (*C*, *R*, *P*)

8. Some cobras are poisonous only if they are snakes. (*C*, *P*, *S*)

9. A poisonous snake is in the zoo. (*P*, *S*, *Z*)

10. A poisonous snake is a deadly creature. (*P*, *S*, *D*, *C*)

8.2 REMOVING AND INTRODUCING QUANTIFIERS

In predicate logic we often wish to make use of the deductive apparatus
of propositional logic in order to construct proofs or derivations of
valid arguments. For example, we might want to invoke simplification to
prove the validity of the argument $(x)(Ax \cdot Bx)$ / $(x)Ax$. But many of
the rules of inference of propositional logic (such as simplification)
may be applied only to whole lines in a proof. Thus, we need rules for
dropping initial quantifiers from quantified propositions. If we remove
quantifiers in the course of constructing a proof, we also eventually
need to add initial quantifiers in order to complete the proof, so we
need rules for doing this, also. Thus, we need rules for both removing
initial quantifiers (*instantiating*) and introducing initial quantifiers
(*generalizing*).

If the quantifier (x) is removed from $(x)(Ax \cdot Bx)$, the result is
$Ax \cdot Bx$. Since x is a variable and not a constant, $Ax \cdot Bx$ makes no
statement at all. (It is to be contrasted with, for instance, $Ac \cdot Bc$,
which says of some named individual c that it is both an A and a B.)
$Ax \cdot Bx$ is what logicians call a *propositional function* or a *statement
function*. Even though it makes no statement, its significance in the
context of a proof may be viewed as corresponding to the statement "Take
any arbitrarily selected individual: *it* is both A and B." Clearly this
statement does follow validly from $(x)(Ax \cdot Bx)$, and it also clearly
entails $(x)(Ax \cdot Bx)$. This perspective on propositional functions helps
explain *universal instantiation* (dropping a universal quantifier) and
universal generalization (adding a universal quantifier).

We have now seen that we can universally instantiate to variables
and universally generalize from them. But how about constants? Well,
if $(x)(Ax \cdot Bx)$ is true and c is some named individual, then clearly
$Ac \cdot Bc$ is true. So we can universally instantiate to constants. Notice,
however, that we cannot universally generalize from a constant: Going
from $Ac \cdot Bc$ to $(x)(Ax \cdot Bx)$ is clearly invalid. Thus, we can universally generalize only from variables, never from constants. We are now
in a position to state the rules for universal instantiation (UI) and
universal generalization (UG).

Let us use the symbol $\mathfrak{F}x$ to denote any propositional function in x,
like Ax, $Ax \cdot Bx$, $Ax \supset {\sim}Bx$, and so on. $\mathfrak{F}y$ will denote the result of
replacing every unquantified-over occurrence of x in $\mathfrak{F}x$ by the variable
y. (Here y may be, but need not be, x.) And $\mathfrak{F}c$ will denote the result
of replacing every unquantified-over occurrence of x in $\mathfrak{F}x$ by the constant c. Then UI can be diagrammatically represented as:

92

UI $\dfrac{(x)\mathcal{F}x}{\mathcal{F}y}$ or $\dfrac{(x)\mathcal{F}x}{\mathcal{F}c}$

Here y is *any variable* and c is *any constant*. Similarly, UG can be represented as:

UG $\dfrac{\mathcal{F}y}{(x)\mathcal{F}x}$

Here y is *any variable* (not a constant). In employing UG, one must be careful to replace *all* the occurrences of y in $\mathcal{F}y$ by x's in $\mathcal{F}x$.

In *existential instantiation* (EI) we want to remove an existential quantifier. It is clearly invalid to conclude from, say, $(\exists x)(Ax \cdot Bx)$ to $Ax \cdot Bx$, so we cannot existentially instantiate to a variable. In instantiating existentially, the idea is that from the claim that there is *something* that is both an A and a B we should be able to conclude that *some* definite thing, even if we do not know what thing it is, is both an A and a B. And we can *name* it—the thing claimed to exist—with a name, say c. Then we can conclude that $Ac \cdot Bc$ is true. In existentially instantiating, then, we are in effect picking a name for some individual, only it is an individual whose identity we do not know. Thus, we can existentially instantiate only to constants. Moreover, the constant we pick as the instantial letter must be a *new* one; that is, it must not have occurred previously in the proof. Otherwise, we would be concluding too much—not merely (and legitimately) that *some* definite thing, which we name, say c, is both A and B, but also (and illegitimately) that this thing is identical with some object to which we have already referred. Thus, the rule for EI can be represented as:

EI $\dfrac{(\exists x)\mathcal{F}x}{\mathcal{F}c}$

Here c is *any constant that has not previously occurred* in the proof.

In *existential generalization* (EG) we want to add an existential quantifier. Clearly it is legitimate to go from $Ac \cdot Bc$ to $(\exists x)(Ax \cdot Bx)$. But moreover, on the mere assumption that anything at all exists, we should also be able to go from $Ay \cdot By$ to $(\exists x)(Ax \cdot Bx)$. So the rule for EG can be represented as:

EG $\dfrac{\mathcal{F}c}{(\exists x)\mathcal{F}x}$ or $\dfrac{\mathcal{F}y}{(\exists x)\mathcal{F}x}$

Here c is *any constant* and y is *any variable*.

In constructing proofs in predicate logic, the typical procedure involves three steps. First, premises are instantiated where necessary. Second, the techniques of propositional logic are applied. Third, the results of the second step are appropriately generalized to reach the conclusion. There are a number of examples of this procedure in the text.

Note that when both existential and universal instantiations are to be done in a proof, the existential instantiations should be performed first; otherwise, the restriction on EI might make it impossible to apply the techniques of propositional logic (see the text for further elucidation of this point). Note also that the rules for dropping and adding quantifiers apply only to whole lines. It is illegitimate to go from, say, $(x)Ax \supset (\exists x)Bx$ to $Ay \supset (\exists x)Bx$, or from $\sim(x)Ax$ to $\sim Ay$. It is also illegitimate to go from, say, $Ac \cdot Bc$ to $(\exists x)Ax \cdot Bc$.

Sample Exercises from Exercise 8.2, Part I

(1) 1. $(x)(Ax \supset Bx)$
    2. $(x)(Bx \supset Cx)$ / $(x)(Ax \supset Cx)$
    3. $Ay \supset By$ 1, UI
    4. $By \supset Cy$ 2, UI
    5. $Ay \supset Cy$ 3, 4, HS
    6. $(x)(Ax \supset Cx)$ 5, UG

(2) 1. $(x)(Bx \supset Cx)$
    2. $(\exists x)(Ax \cdot Bx)$ / $(\exists x)(Ax \cdot Cx)$
    3. $Ac \cdot Bc$ 2, EI
    4. Ac 3, Simp
    5. $Bc \cdot Ac$ 3, Com
    6. Bc 5, Simp
    7. $Bc \supset Cc$ 1, UI
    8. Cc 6, 7, MP
    9. $Ac \cdot Cc$ 4, 8, Conj
   10. $(\exists x)(Ax \cdot Cx)$ 9, EG

(3) 1. $(x)(Ax \supset Bx)$
    2. $\sim Bm$ / $(\exists x) \sim Ax$
    3. $Am \supset Bm$ 1, UI
    4. $\sim Am$ 2, 3, MT
    5. $(\exists x) \sim Ax$ 4, EG

(4) 1. $(x)[Ax \supset (Bx \lor Cx)]$
    2. $Ag \cdot \sim Bg$ / Cg
    3. Ag 2, Simp
    4. $\sim Bg \cdot Ag$ 2, Com
    5. $\sim Bg$ 4, Simp
    6. $Ag \supset (Bg \lor Cg)$ 1, UI
    7. $Bg \lor Cg$ 3, 6, MP
    8. Cg 5, 7, DS

Additional Exercises for Section 8.2

Using the rules for dropping and adding quantifiers and the rules of
inference of propositional logic, but without using CP or IP, construct proofs for the following arguments.

(1) 1. $(x)(Ax \supset Bx)$
    2. $(x)(Bx \supset Cx)$
    3. $(x)(Cx \supset Dx)$ / $(x)(\sim Dx \supset \sim Ax)$

(2) 1. $(x)(Ax \cdot Bx)$
    2. $(\exists x)Ax \supset (\exists x)Cx$ / $(\exists x)Cx$

(3) 1. $(\exists x)(Ax \cdot Bx)$ / $(\exists x)Ax \cdot (\exists x)Bx$

(4) 1. $(x)Ax \lor (x)Bx$
    2. $(x)Ax \supset (x)Cx$
    3. $\sim(x)Cx$ / $(\exists x)Bx$

94

(5) 1. $(\exists x)(Ax \lor Bx)$
    2. $(x) \sim Ax$
    3. $(\exists x)Bx \supset (x)Cx$ / $(x)(Cx \lor Dx)$

(6) 1. $(x)[(Ax \cdot Bx) \lor Cx]$
    2. $(\exists x) \sim Bx$ / $(\exists x)Cx$

(7) 1. $(x)[Ax \supset (Bx \supset Cx)]$
    2. $(\exists x)(Ax \lor Dx)$
    3. $(x) \sim Dx$
    4. $(x)Bx$ / $(\exists x)Cx$

(8) 1. $(x)(Ax \supset Bx)$
    2. $(x)Ax$ / $(x)Bx$

(9) 1. $(\exists x)(Ax \cdot Bx)$
    2. $(x)[Bx \supset (Dx \cdot Ex)]$
    3. $(x)(Ex \supset \sim Fx)$ / $(\exists x) \sim Fx$

(10) 1. $(x)(Ax \supset Bx)$
    2. $(x)(\sim Bx \lor Cx)$
    3. $(\exists x)Ax$
    4. $(x) \sim Cx$ / $(x)Ax$

8.3 CHANGE OF QUANTIFIER RULES

Propositions with negation signs before quantifiers may easily be changed
to logically equivalent propositions without negation signs before their
quantifiers: The negation sign is moved from its initial position to
the propositional function governed by the quantifier and the quantifier
is changed to its opposite. This may be expressed in the following rules,
called collectively the *change of quantifier rules* (CQ):

    CQ $\sim(x)\mathcal{F}x$ is logically equivalent to $(\exists x) \sim \mathcal{F}x$
          $\sim(x) \sim \mathcal{F}x$ is logically equivalent to $(\exists x)\mathcal{F}x$
          $\sim(\exists x)\mathcal{F}x$ is logically equivalent to $(x) \sim \mathcal{F}x$
          $\sim(\exists x) \sim \mathcal{F}x$ is logically equivalent to $(x)\mathcal{F}x$

These rules may, of course, be used in either direction, and they need
not be applied only to whole lines.

Sample Exercises from Exercise 8.3, Part I

(1) 1. $(x)Ax \supset (\exists x)Bx$
    2. $(x) \sim Bx$ / $(\exists x) \sim Ax$
    3. $\sim(\exists x) \sim \sim Bx$ 2, CQ
    4. $\sim(\exists x)Bx$ 3, DN
    5. $\sim(x)Ax$ 1, 4, MT
    6. $(\exists x) \sim Ax$ 5, CQ

(2) 1. $(\exists x) \sim Ax \lor (\exists x) \sim Bx$
    2. $(x)Bx$ / $\sim(x)Ax$
    3. $\sim(\exists x) \sim Bx$ 2, CQ
    4. $(\exists x) \sim Bx \lor (\exists x) \sim Ax$ 1, Com

95

5. $(\exists x) \sim Ax$ 3, 4, DS
6. $\sim(x) \sim {\sim} Ax$ 5, CQ
7. $\sim(x)Ax$ 6, DN

8.4 CONDITIONAL AND INDIRECT PROOF

The use of conditional and indirect proof in predicate logic is basically the same as for propositional logic. The format is entirely the same. When the antecedent and consequent of the proposition to be established by conditional proof are whole propositions—not propositional functions—the use of conditional or indirect proof presents no special problems. Sometimes, however, it is desirable to employ conditional proof in such a way that the antecedent of the conditional to be established is not a whole statement but rather a statement function. For example, in order to prove valid the argument $(x)[Ax \supset (Bx \cdot Cx)]$ / $(x)(Ax \supset Bx)$, one would like to be able to assume Ax, to deduce Bx from this assumption and the premise, and then to discharge the assumption and universally generalize to the conclusion. In using CP in this manner, however, we must be careful to observe a special restriction on universal generalization: In the scope of an assumption, UG must not be used to generalize on a variable that occurs in that assumption ungoverned by a quantifier.

The basic reason for this restriction on UG is that we do not want to be able to derive lines like $Ax \supset (x)Ax$ merely by assuming Ax. To allow such lines is tantamount to allowing obviously invalid arguments to be proved as valid. For example, consider the argument $(\exists x)Ax$ / $(x)Ax$. It is obviously invalid. But without the restriction on UG, we could derive its validity easily, as follows:

1. $(\exists x)Ax$ / $(x)Ax$
   2. $\sim Ax$ CP
   3. $(x) \sim Ax$ 2, UG (invalid)
4. $\sim Ax \supset (x) \sim Ax$ 2-3, CP
5. $\sim(x) \sim Ax$ 1, CQ
6. $\sim {\sim} Ax$ 4, 5, MT
7. Ax 6, DN
8. $(x)Ax$ 7, UG

Since indirect proof is only a special case of conditional proof, the restriction on UG also extends to IP. A variable is not to be generalized upon inside the scope of an IP assumption if that variable occurs in that assumption ungoverned by a quantifier. Here is an example of the derivation of the same invalid argument as above by a faulty use of UG inside the scope of an assumption introduced by IP:

1. $(\exists x)Ax$ / $(x)Ax$
   2. $\sim Ax$ IP
   3. $(x) \sim Ax$ 2, UG (invalid)
   4. $\sim(\exists x)Ax$ 3, CQ
   5. $(\exists x)Ax \cdot \sim(\exists x)Ax$ 1, 4, Conj
6. Ax 2-5, IP
7. $(x)Ax$ 6, UG

(1) 1. $(x)(Ax \supset Bx)$

   2. $(x)(Ax \supset Cx)$ / $(x)[Ax \supset (Bx \cdot Cx)]$

      3. Ax CP

      4. $Ax \supset Bx$ 1, UI

      5. $Ax \supset Cx$ 2, UI

      6. Bx 3, 4, MP

      7. Cx 3, 5, MP

      8. $Bx \cdot Cx$ 6, 7, Conj

   9. $Ax \supset (Bx \cdot Cx)$ 3-8, CP

  10. $(x)[Ax \supset (Bx \cdot Cx)]$ 9, UG

(2) 1. $(\exists x)Ax \supset (\exists x)(Bx \cdot Cx)$

   2. $(\exists x)(Cx \vee Dx) \supset (x)Ex$ / $(x)(Ax \supset Ex)$

      3. Ax CP

      4. $(\exists x)Ax$ 3, EG

      5. $(\exists x)(Bx \cdot Cx)$ 1, 4, MP

      6. $Bc \cdot Cc$ 5, EI

      7. $Cc \cdot Bc$ 6, Com

      8. Cc 7, Simp

      9. $Cc \vee Dc$ 8, Add

    10. $(\exists x)(Cx \vee Dx)$ 9, EG

    11. $(x)Ex$ 2, 10, MP

    12. Ex 11, UI

  13. $Ax \supset Ex$ 3-12, CP

  14. $(x)(Ax \supset Ex)$ 13, UG

(3) 1. $(\exists x)Ax \supset (\exists x)(Bx \cdot Cx)$

   2. $\sim(\exists x)Cx$ / $(x) \sim Ax$

      3. $\sim(x) \sim Ax$ IP

      4. $(\exists x)Ax$ 3, CQ

      5. $(\exists x)(Bx \cdot Cx)$ 1, 4, MP

      6. $Bc \cdot Cc$ 5, EI

      7. $Cc \cdot Bc$ 6, Com

      8. Cc 7, Simp

      9. $(\exists x)Cx$ 8, EG

    10. $(\exists x)Cx \cdot \sim(\exists x)Cx$ 2, 9, Conj

  11. $(x) \sim Ax$ 3-10, IP

(4) 1. $(x)(Ax \supset Cx)$

   2. $(\exists x)Cx \supset (\exists x)(Bx \cdot Dx)$ / $(\exists x)Ax \supset (\exists x)Bx$

      3. $(\exists x)Ax$ CP

      4. Ac 3, EI

      5. $Ac \supset Cc$ 1, UI

      6. Cc 4, 5, MP

      7. $(\exists x)Cx$ 6, EG

      8. $(\exists x)(Bx \cdot Dx)$ 2, 7, MP

      9. $Ba \cdot Da$ 8, EI

    10. Ba 9, Simp

    11. $(\exists x)Bx$ 10, EG

  12. $(\exists x)Ax \supset (\exists x)Bx$ 3-11, CP

Additional Exercises for Section 8.4

Use CP or IP in proving the following arguments valid.

(1) 1. $(\exists x)Ax \supset (x)Bx$
    2. $(\exists x)Bx \supset (x)Cx$ / $(x)Ax \supset (x)Cx$

(2) 1. $(x)[(Ax \lor Bx) \supset (Cx \cdot Dx)]$ / $(x)(Ax \supset Cx)$

(3) 1. $(\exists x)Ax \supset (x)(Bx \cdot Cx)$ / $(x)(Ax \supset Cx)$

(4) 1. $(\exists x)(Ax \lor Bx) \supset (x)(Cx \cdot Dx)$
    2. $(x)(Bx \supset Dx) \supset (x)Ex$ / $(\exists x)Ex$

(5) 1. $(x)[(Bx \cdot Cx) \lor Ax]$
    2. $(x)[Bx \supset (Dx \cdot \sim Ex)]$
    3. $(x)(Ax \supset Fx)$ / $(x)(Ex \supset Fx)$

8.5   PROVING INVALIDITY

One standard technique for proving the invalidity of an argument in predicate logic consists in finding an interpretation of the propositions in the argument such that all the premises of the argument turn out true and the conclusion turns out false.

Interpretation of a proposition of predicate logic means designating some *universe of discourse*, which the proposition is then understood to be about, and then assigning a meaning in this universe for each of the predicates in the proposition. When this is done, the proposition can be explicated as meaning a certain thing about the universe, and it can be assigned a truth value. Let us proceed to see how this is done.

A universe may consist of one or more individuals. Suppose a universe consists of three named individuals a, b, and c. Then for any universally quantified proposition $(x)Fx$, its meaning with respect to this universe is, rather clearly, $Fa \cdot Fb \cdot Fc$. Moreover, any existentially quantified proposition $(\exists x)Fx$ has the following meaning with respect to this universe:

$$Fa \lor Fb \lor Fc$$

A predicate may be assigned a meaning for a universe by designating a truth value for its application to each individual in the universe. Furthermore, assigning such a meaning to all the predicates of a proposition will determine a truth value for that proposition.

Suppose, for example, that the universe has two members, a and b, and that for some predicate, for example P, Pa is true and Pb is false. Then the statement $(x)Px$ reduces to $Pa \cdot Pb$, which is false, and the statement $(\exists x)Px$ reduces to $Pa \lor Pb$, which is true.

For any invalid argument of predicate logic, at least one universe and assignment of meaning to all the predicates will make all the premises true and the conclusion false.

Sample Exercises from Exercise 8.5, Part I

(1) Let the universe consist of one individual a, and let $Aa = F$, $Ba = T$, and $Ca = F$. Then the argument has the meaning

98

1. $Aa \supset Ba$
2. $Aa \supset Ca$ / $Ba \supset Ca$

As the following truth table shows, this makes all the premises true and the conclusion false:

$$Aa \supset Ba \quad / \quad Aa \supset Ca \quad // \quad Ba \supset Ca$$
$$\text{F} \boxed{\text{T}} \text{F} \qquad \text{F} \boxed{\text{T}} \text{F} \qquad \text{T} \boxed{\text{F}} \text{F}$$

(2) Let the universe consist of two individuals n and a. (Note that n is included because it is mentioned in the argument.) Now let Aa = T, Ba = F, An = F, and Bn = T. With this universe, the argument has the meaning

1. $(Aa \lor Ba) \cdot (An \lor Bn)$
2. $\sim An$ / $Ba \cdot Bn$

As the following truth table shows, this makes all the premises true and the conclusion false:

$$(Aa \lor Ba) \cdot (An \lor Bn) \quad / \sim An \quad // \quad Ba \cdot Bn$$
$$\text{T T F} \quad \boxed{\text{T}} \quad \text{F T T} \qquad \boxed{\text{T}} \text{F} \qquad \text{F} \boxed{\text{F}} \text{T}$$

Additional Exercises for Section 8.5

Prove that the following arguments are invalid by constructing a universe and a meaning assignment for the predicates that makes the premise true and the conclusion false.

(1) 1. $(\exists x)(Ax \cdot Bx)$ / $(x)Bx$

(2) 1. $(x)(Ax \supset Bx)$
    2. $(\exists x)(Ax \cdot Cx)$ / $(x)Bx$

(3) 1. $(x)[Ax \supset (Bx \cdot Cx)]$
    2. $(x)(Cx \supset Dx)$ / $(x)(Dx \supset Ax)$

(4) 1. $(x)Ax \supset (x)Bx$ / $(x)(Ax \supset Bx)$

(5) 1. $(x)(Ax \supset Bx)$ / $(\exists x)(Ax \equiv Bx)$

8.6 RELATIONAL PREDICATES AND OVERLAPPING QUANTIFIERS

The logical apparatus of predicate logic can be extended to cover the logic of binary relations (such as a is a friend of b), trinary relations (such as a is between b and c), and relations of higher order. Symbolically, such relations can be expressed by a capital letter followed by lower case letters representing the items related: for example, Fab can be used to express that a is a friend of b, and $Babc$ can be used to express that a is between b and c. As the latter example shows, the order of the lower case letters following the capital letter is important.

    The use of variables and quantifiers with relational predicates is a natural extension of their use with nonrelational predicates. Thus, $(x)Fxa$ means that everything is a friend of a, and $(\exists x)Bxab$ means that something is between a and b. With relational predicates, however, there is the possibility of using variables in more than one position, and there is the possibility of multiple and overlapping quantification. Thus, we have such symbolic statements as:

$(x)(y)Fxy$, which means: for all x and for all y, x is a friend of y

$(x)(\exists y)Fxy$, which means: for all x there is some y such that x is a friend of y

$(\exists x)(y)Fxy$, which means: there is some x such that for all y, x is a friend of y

$(\exists x)(\exists y)Fxy$, which means: there is an x and there is a y such that x is a friend of y

Note that when quantifiers are mixed in type, as in the second and third of these examples, the order of the quantifiers makes a crucial difference in meaning.

The apparatus of quantifiers and relational and nonrelational predicates can be combined with that of propositional logic to provide a system for translating an extensive variety of complex statements. For example, if P stands for the predicate of personhood and F for the binary relation of friendship, we can perform the following translations:

Everyone has some friend: $(x)[Px \supset (\exists y)Fyx]$
Someone has everyone as a friend: $(\exists x)[Px \cdot (y)(Py \supset Fyx)]$
No one has anyone as a friend: $(x)[Px \supset (y)(Py \supset \sim Fyx)]$
Anyone who has a friend has himself as a friend:
$(x)[(Px \cdot (\exists y)Fyx) \supset Fxx]$

Students often find that constructing such translations is difficult. The text provides many helpful pointers about translation, but there is simply no substitute for practice.

The rules of inference for nonrelational predicate logic apply, with only minor alteration, to the logic of relational predicates and multiple, overlapping quantifiers. One point to keep in mind in using CQ is that each quantifier of an overlapping series is understood to govern the entire string of symbols to its right. Thus, $(x)(\exists y)(z)Bxyz$ is understood to mean $(x)\{(\exists y)[(z)Bxyz]\}$. Therefore, $\sim(x)(\exists y)(z)Bxyz$ is logically equivalent to $(\exists x)\sim\{(\exists y)[(z)Bxyz]\}$, and thus to $(\exists x)(y)\sim[(z)Bxyz]$, and thus to $(\exists x)(y)(\exists z)\sim Bxyz$.

A second point to keep in mind concerns the rules for dropping and adding quantifiers: we must add an additional restriction to UG in order to prevent the possibility of deriving certain types of invalid arguments. The argument $(x)(\exists y)Pxy$ / $(\exists y)(x)Pxy$ is clearly invalid. (To see this, consider Pxy to mean that x is a number greater than the number y; then the premise says that for every number there is a greater one, and the conclusion says that there is a greatest number; clearly this inference is wrong.) Without some restriction on UG, we could carry out the following derivation:

1. $(x)(\exists y)Pxy$
2. $(\exists y)Pxy$ 1, UI
3. Pxc 2, EI
4. $(x)Pxc$ 3, UG (invalid)
5. $(\exists y)(x)Pxy$ 4, EG

100

The basic reason step 4 is invalid is that the "choice" of c in line 3 is dependent on x's already having been specified, whereas in line 4 it is made to appear as if c is independent of the specification of x. To prevent such inferences as line 4, then, we need the following restriction on UG: UG must not be used if the line being generalized upon by UG contains a constant obtained from EI (a so-called existential name) and if the variable being generalized upon is ungoverned by a quantifier in the line where that constant was introduced by the EI step.

Conditional and indirect proof are used the same way with relational predicates as with nonrelational predicates; the crucial point to keep in mind is the restriction on UG that must be observed inside the scope of assumptions.

A final point of caution must be mentioned with regard to universal instantiation: When a variable is introduced by UI into a proof, this variable must not be identical to the variable of a quantifier within whose governance its introduced occurrence falls. The following "proof" illustrates an incorrect use of UI:

1. $(x)(\exists y)Pxy$
2. $(\exists y)Pyy$ 1, UI (invalid)

If the variable introduced into line 2 were not y but some other variable, say x or z, the instantiation would be correct.

It is important that in using UG or EG the quantifiers capture only the variables they are intended to capture. They should not capture variables that are already bound by other quantifiers, and they should not capture other free variables in the statement function. These qualifications rule out such invalid inferences as:

1. $(\exists x)Pxy$
2. $(x)(\exists x)Pxx$ 1, UG (invalid)

Care should also be taken to avoid inferences such as:

1. $(\exists x)Pxc$
2. $(\exists x)(\exists x)Pxx$ 1, EG (invalid)

and

1. $(x)(\exists y)(Fx \equiv {\sim}Fy)$
2. $(\exists x)(Fx \equiv {\sim}Fy)$ 1, UI
3. $Fx \equiv {\sim}Fc$ 2, EI
4. $(\exists x)(Fx \equiv {\sim}Fx)$ 3, EG (invalid)

Sample Exercises from Exercise 8.6, Part I

1. Charmaine read *Paradise Lost*.

    Rcp

2. Whoever reads *Paradise Lost* is educated.

    $(x)[(Px \cdot Rxp) \supset Ex]$ Note: $Px = x$ is a person

3. James is a friend of either Ellen or Connie.

    $Fje \lor Fjc$

4. If James has any friends, then Marlene is one of them.

$(\exists x)Fxj \supset Fmj$

Sample Exercises from Exercise 8.6, Part II

(1) 1. $(x)[Ax \supset (y)Bxy]$
    2. Am / $(y)Bmy$
    3. $Am \supset (y)Bmy$ 1, UI
    4. $(y)Bmy$ 2, 3, MP

(2) 1. $(x)[Ax \supset (y)(By \supset Cxy)]$
    2. $Am \cdot Bn$ / Cmn
    3. $Am \supset (y)(By \supset Cmy)$ 1, UI
    4. Am 2, Simp
    5. $(y)(By \supset Cmy)$ 3, 4, MP
    6. $Bn \cdot Am$ 2, Com
    7. Bn 6, Simp
    8. $Bn \supset Cmn$ 5, UI
    9. Cmn 7, 8, MP

(3) 1. $(\exists x)[Ax \cdot (y)(By \supset Cxy)]$
    2. $(\exists x)Ax \supset Bj$ / $(\exists x)Cxj$
    3. $Ac \cdot (y)(By \supset Ccy)$ 1, EI
    4. Ac 3, Simp
    5. $(\exists x)Ax$ 4, EG
    6. Bj 2, 5, MP
    7. $(y)(By \supset Ccy) \cdot Ac$ 3, Com
    8. $(y)(By \supset Ccy)$ 7, Simp
    9. $Bj \supset Ccj$ 8, UI
   10. Ccj 6, 9, MP
   11. $(\exists x)Cxj$ 10, EG

(4) 1. $(x)(\exists y)(Ax \supset By)$ / $(x)Ax \supset (\exists y)By$
    2. $(x)Ax$ CP
    3. $(\exists y)(Ax \supset By)$ 1, UI
    4. $Ax \supset Bc$ 3, EI
    5. Ax 2, UI
    6. Bc 4, 5, MP
    7. $(\exists y)By$ 6, EG
    8. $(x)Ax \supset (\exists y)By$ 2-7, CP

Additional Exercises for Section 8.6

I. Translate the following statements into symbolic propositions,
    using the following predicates and relations: Px = x is a person;
    Txy = x is taller than y; Lxy = x likes y.

    1. No one is taller than John.

    2. No one is taller than himself.

    3. Everyone likes somebody.

    4. No one likes everybody.

5. No one is liked by everybody.

6. Everyone likes at least one person who is taller than he.

7. There is somebody who likes anyone who is taller than he.

8. No one likes anyone who is not taller than he.

9. Everyone does not like at least one person who is taller than he.

10. If everyone likes anybody who is not taller than he, then everyone likes himself.

II. Prove the following symbolized arguments valid.

(1) 1. $(x)(\exists y)Fxy \supset (x)Gxx$
    2. $(\exists y)(x)Fxy$ / $(x)Gxx$

(2) 1. $(x)(y)Fxy$ / $(\exists z)Fzz$

(3) 1. $(x)(y)(Fxy \cdot Gyx)$ / $(z)(Fzz \cdot Gzz)$

(4) 1. $(x)[Fx \supset (y)Gy]$ / $(\exists x)Fx \supset (\exists y)Gy$

(5) 1. $(x)Fx \cdot (y)Gy$ / $(x)(y)(Fx \cdot Gy)$

(6) 1. $(x)(\exists y)Ixy$
    2. $(x)(y)(Ixy \supset \sim Mxy)$ / $(x)(\exists y) \sim Mxy$

(7) 1. $(x)(y)(z)[Bxyz \supset (Lxy \cdot Lyz)]$
    2. $(x)(y)(Lxy \supset \sim Ixy)$ / $(x)(y)(z)[Bxyz \supset \sim(Ixy \lor Iyz)]$

(8) 1. $(x)(y)(z)[Bxyz \supset (Lxy \cdot Lyz)]$
    2. $(x)Ixx$
    3. $(x)(y)(Ixy \supset \sim Lxy)$ / $(x)(y) \sim Bxxy$

(9) 1. $(x)(y)(Lxy \lor Lyx)$
    2. $(x)(y)[(Lxy \cdot Lyx) \supset Ixy]$ / $(x)(y)[\sim Ixy \supset (Lxy \equiv \sim Lyx)]$

(10) 1. $(x)(y)(z)[(Lxy \cdot Lyz) \supset Lxz]$
    2. $(x)(y)(Lxy \supset Lyx)$ /$(x)[(\exists y)Lxy \supset Lxx]$

9
INDUCTION

9.1 CAUSALITY AND MILL'S METHODS

The notion of causation is to some extent ambiguous. When we say that A is the cause of B or a cause of B, we can mean that A is a necessary condition of B, that A is a sufficient condition of B, or that A is both a necessary and sufficient condition of B. There are deep philosophical difficulties concerning the relation between asserting causal connections among particular events and asserting general causal statements about types of events. These difficulties will be largely ignored here. When events A and B are spoken of, it will usually be clear when *particular* events are being discussed and when *types* of events are being discussed.

When cause as necessary condition and cause as sufficient condition are distinguished, Mill's methods of identifying causes can be broken down into a more refined classification than Mill himself presented. The more refined classification is presented here.

The *direct method of agreement* is a method for identifying a cause in the sense of a necessary condition. To use it, examine all cases in which a given effect E is presented and try to find some factor F that is present in all these cases. That is to say, eliminate any factor that is not present in all of the cases. Any factor F that remains is a candidate for a necessary condition of E and consequently may be a cause of E in this sense.

The *inverse method of agreement* is a method for identifying a cause in the sense of a sufficient condition. To use it, examine all cases in which a given effect E is absent and try to find some factor F that is also absent. Eliminate any factor that is present whenever E is absent. Any factor that remains will be such that its nonpresence may be a necessary condition of the nonpresence of E. In other words, then, the presence of this factor may be a sufficient condition for the presence of E and consequently may be a cause of E in this sense.

The *double method of agreement* is simply a combination of the direct method of agreement and the inverse method of agreement. To use it, examine all cases in which a given effect E is present and all cases in which it is absent. Try to find a factor F that is present when E is present and absent when E is absent. This factor, if it exists, may be a necessary and sufficient condition for E and thus may be a cause of it in this sense.

The *method of difference* consists in examining two cases (or classes of cases), one of which exhibits an effect E and the other of which does not. To use it, try to find a single factor F that is present in the case(s) in which E is present and absent in the case(s) in which E is absent. The factor F is a candidate for what differentiates the two cases (or classes of cases). It is then a candidate for a cause in the sense of a sufficient condition.

The *joint method of agreement and difference* consists in combining the direct method of agreement with the method of difference. The result is a candidate for a cause in the sense of a necessary and sufficient condition.

The *method of residues* consists in "subtracting" known causal connections from other, more complex, known causal relations, leaving as a candidate for a causal connection the remaining relation. If there is a causal connection between a complex or conjunctive event A and another such event B, and if event a is an isolatable part or conjunct of event A, and b is an isolatable part or conjunct of event B, and if there is a known causal relation between a and b, then it can be concluded that there is a probable causal connection between the residue $A - a$ and the residue $B - b$. (The nature of the subtraction here is, of course, somewhat unclear.)

The *method of concomitant variation* consists in identifying a functional relation (perhaps expressible as an equation) between a factor F that admits of quantity or degree and a factor E that admits of quantity or degree, such that variations in the quantity of F correspond with variations in the quantity of E. This functional relation may be direct or inverse. When such a relation is found, it may be concluded that F and E are probably causally related.

Sample Exercises from Exercise 9.1, Part I

1. Throwing a brick through a window will cause the window to break.

   This is a statement of a *sufficient* condition for the window to break. Obviously, throwing a brick is not necessary for the window to break.

2. Heating an iron rod causes it to expand.

   This is a statement of a sufficient condition for the iron rod to expand. Under normal conditions it is also necessary, but in general it is not a necessary condition: an iron rod will expand under certain sorts of magnetic fields, when great pressure is taken off it, and so forth.

Exercises for Section 9.1

Identify the Mills method that is being employed in each of the following inferences.

1. Virus V was found in every case of sinusitis that we examined. We conclude, then, that virus V is a cause of sinusitis.

2. We have never found a disturbed home life in the background of any of our students who do not have trouble in school. We may conclude, then, that a disturbed home life is a cause of student trouble in school.

3. We compared two classes of rats, one with stunted growth and one without stunted growth. The stunted rats had an unusual amount of calcium in their early diets, whereas the nonstunted rats had early diets with a normal amount of calcium. We concluded that abnormal amounts of calcium in the early diet of rats is a cause of stunting in their growth.

4. We notice that a rise in elevation is correlated with a fall in the level of mercury in a barometer. We conclude that the elevation above sea level determines the height of mercury in a barometer.

5. Plants with root rot are always found to be heavily watered. We have never seen a plant without root rot that was heavily watered. It can be concluded, then, that heavy watering of plants causes them to have root rot.

9.2 PROBABILITY

The notion of probability, like that of causality, is crucial for the study of induction. But like causality, probability can have different meanings. For example, if we refer to the probability of drawing a spade from a standard deck of cards, we have in mind the mathematical procedure of comparing the thirteen spades in a standard deck to the fifty-two cards; but if we refer to the probability that a meteor of gigantic size collided with the earth millions of years ago, we have in mind something very different from such a mathematical procedure.

Different meanings of probability can be correlated with different theories or interpretations of probability. There are, for example, the classical theory, the relative-frequency theory, and the subjectivist theory of probability, each of which is discussed in the text. These theories of probability have in common what is known as *the probability calculus*. The probability calculus is a set of mathematical formulas for computing probabilities. It is usually represented by a set of axioms and the theorems that follow logically from these axioms. But the content of the probability calculus is perhaps best explained in conjunction with an account of the classical theory.

The *classical theory* begins with the idea of an experiment that can have n discrete possible outcomes. According to the *principle of indifference*, each outcome is equally likely; in other words, the n outcomes are equiprobable. Moreover, the outcomes of an experiment can be classified into types. Then, the probability that the result of the experiment will be an outcome of type A is defined by the formula

$$P(A) = f/n,$$

where f is the number of outcomes of type A. For example, the probability of drawing a spade from a standard deck is $13/52 = 1/4$, since there are 52 equiprobable outcomes, 13 of which are spades.

Since outcomes are of various types, we may consider the outcomes of logically combining given types. For example, we may consider the probability that the result of an experiment is *not* of type A, the probability that the result is both of type A and of type B, and so forth. The probability calculus enables us to compute such probabilities. For example, the probability that a result is not of type A is computed by the *negation rule* to be

106

$$P(\text{not-}A) = (n - f)/n = 1 - f/n = 1 - P(A)$$

Clearly, the probability of a result of a type that *necessarily* results, such as "A or not-A," is 1; and the probability of a result of a type that cannot happen, such as "A and not-A," is 0.

Computing probabilities of conjunctive types is a bit more complicated. When two types are *independent* of each other (that is, when an occurrence of the one type has no influence one way or the other on the probability of an occurrence of the other type), the *restricted conjunction rule* may be used to compute the probability of the conjunction of the two types:

$$P(A \text{ and } B) = P(A) \times P(B)$$

Alternatively, the restricted conjunction rule may be used as a definition of the independence of two event types.

When two event types are not independent of each other, we must use the *general conjunction rule*. This rule involves an expression that quantifies the degree of influence that one event type has on the other: $P(B \text{ given } A)$. The meaning of this term is "the probability that B occurs *given that A* occurs (or has occurred)." The general conjunction rule, then, is

$$P(A \text{ and } B) = P(A) \times P(B \text{ given } A)$$

When two event types are mutually exclusive, the probability that the result of an experiment is one or the other of these types, written $P(A \text{ or } B)$, is given by the *restricted disjunction rule*:

$$P(A \text{ or } B) = P(A) + P(B)$$

When two event types are not mutually exclusive, the probability that the result of the experiment is one or the other (or both) of these types is given by the *general disjunction rule*:

$$P(A \text{ or } B) = P(A) + P(B) - P(A \text{ and } B)$$

The above rules for calculating probabilities constitute the core of the probability calculus. The same calculus can also be associated with theories of probability other than the classical theory, although the association is more complicated to explain, and will be omitted here in favor of a brief exposition of the basic ideas of the relative-frequency theory and the subjectivist theory.

With the *relative-frequency theory*, an experiment of a given type, and that has various outcomes of given types, is performed repeatedly, while observations are made of the type of outcome resulting from each performance of the experiment. After n_0 such performances, f_0 outcomes of type A are observed. The probability of an outcome of type A is then computed as

$$P(A) = n_0/f_0$$

Clearly, $P(A)$ may be computed differently, depending on the number of performances of the experiment. But typically as n_0 gets larger and larger, $P(A)$ begins to settle about some fixed value; that is, $P(A)$ differs from this fixed value by smaller and smaller amounts. We may say, then, that the probability of A is this fixed, limiting value of the relative frequency n_o/f_o as n_o increases indefinitely.

According to the *subjectivist theory* of probability, a probability number (that is, a number between zero and one) is assigned to various types of outcomes of a given type of experiment. The assignment is made by some person on the basis of his or her subjective expectation of the likelihood that an outcome of a given type will occur. The main point of subjectivist theory is that if the subjective assignments are not made consistently with the probability calculus, then those assignments are irrational in the following sense: a bet or wager may be made with the person which he or she is bound to lose. Subjectivist probability theory is helpful in analyzing assignments of probability to one-of-a-kind situations.

Sample Exercises from Exercise 9.2, Part I

1. The probability of rolling a five on a single die is 1/6. There is one way to roll a five out of six possible outcomes.

2. If 273 Ajax trucks out of a possible 9,750 developed transmission problems within the first two years of operation, then the probability that an Ajax truck will develop transmission problems within the first two years is 273/9,750.

Exercises for Section 9.2

Compute the following probabilities.

1. The probability of not drawing a king in a draw from a standard deck of cards.

2. The probability of drawing both a king and a spade.

3. The probability of drawing a king or a spade or both.

4. The probability of drawing a king given that a spade is drawn.

5. The probability of not drawing a king given that a spade is not drawn.

6. The probability of drawing a face card.

7. The probability of rolling a total of seven on a single roll of a pair of standard dice.

8. The probability of rolling a total of either two or twelve.

9. The probability of throwing a roll such that one or the other of the dice shows a six, given that a total of seven is thrown.

10. The probability of neither die showing a four given that a total of six is rolled.

Many difficulties exist with regard to statistical reasoning. Five areas of difficulty are identified and discussed in the text.

1. *Samples*. Generalizations based on samples should be made only when the sample is randomly selected and large enough. In addition, attributing characteristics to members of a sample should be free of bias on the part of the persons attributing those characteristics.

2. *The Meaning of Average*. The word "average" may mean various things:

a. The *mean*—the sum of the individual values of the data divided by the number of data in the set.
b. The *median*—the mid-point of the data values when they are arranged in a linear order according to value.
c. The *mode*—the particular data value occurring with the greatest frequency.

Confusing these very different averages can result in misguided conclusions, as the text shows.

3. *Dispersion*. This term refers to how widely spaced or spread out the values of the data are. Ignoring dispersion in statistical descriptions of data can lead to mistaken conclusions, as the text shows.

4. *Graphs and Pictograms*. Such representations can mislead, as the text shows, because of suggestive scaling of graph axes, because of the omission (or chopping off) of portions of the axes, or because of incorrectly proportioned illustrations.

5. *Percentages*. Percentages, for example percentage differences, should always be given with a clear *base* of comparison. If this is not done, the meaning of the percentage is undeterminable.

Sample Exercises from Exercise 9.3, Part I

1. To test the algae content in a lake, a biologist took a sample of the water at one end. The algae in the sample registered 5 micrograms per liter. Therefore, the algae in the lake at that time registered 5 micrograms per liter.

    The conclusion is based on a sample that is not likely to be representative.

2. To estimate public support for a new municipality-funded convention center, researchers surveyed 100 homeowners in one of the city's fashionable neighborhoods. They found that 89 percent of those sampled were enthusiastic about the project. Therefore, we may conclude that 89 percent of the city's residents favor the convention center.

    The conclusion is based on a nonrepresentative sample.

Identify the area of statistical difficulty that casts doubt on the following statistical reasonings:

1. Brand X acne medicine is 76 percent better than its best competitor. Thus, you should buy Brand X.

2. Of the ministers surveyed, 80 percent said they would vote Republican in the election. So the Republicans will win overwhelmingly.

3. The average income—mean, median, and mode—in this neighborhood is $50,000 per year. We may conclude that most of the people in it are solidly middle class.

4. When slave owners asked slaves if they wanted to be free, an overwhelming number of them said they preferred to remain slaves. Clearly, then, freeing the slaves was something that took place against their will.

5. The average age of the students in this class is 19.6 years. So there must be at least several students in this class between 19 and 20 years of age.

9.4 HYPOTHETICAL REASONING

Hypothetical reasoning is inferring from a set of data to a hypothesis that explains these data. Once a hypothesis has been formulated, it may be tested against the data it is supposed to explain. It also may be tested by using it to predict new data and then seeing whether the prediction is correct.

For a hypothesis to be acceptable, it must at least be internally consistent and coherent. *Coherent* means that the hypothesis must be so constituted internally that its basic concepts and assertions do not raise insuperable problems, or more problems than the hypothesis was invented to solve. Also, a hypothesis must be adequate. That is, it must be able to explain the data that it was invented to explain.

The most elementary form of hypothetical reasoning is generalization. But historically, the most interesting and fruitful hypotheses, both in the sciences and in philosophy, have involved great intuitive, creative leaps of imagination. Obviously, then, the logic of hypothesis construction—if there is such a logic—is a matter of great complexity. As a matter of fact, this whole topic is a matter of spirited controversy. Much about hypothetical reasoning can be learned simply by studying the history of the sciences and of philosophy.

ANSWERS TO ADDITIONAL EXERCISES

CHAPTER 1

<u>1.1</u>

1. P: Cigarette smoking is a leading cause of cancer.
   C: Only a fool or a daredevil smokes cigarettes.

2. P_1: If we had world enough and time, this coyness would not be a crime.
   P_2: We don't have world enough and time.
   C: This coyness is a crime.

3. P: The square root of the number two is an irrational number.
   C: The hypotenuse of an isosceles right triangle is not commensurable with its side.

4. P_1: No man is an island.
   P_2: Every man is a piece of the continent.
   P_3: Every man is a part of the main.
   C: No one should send to know for whom the bell tolls.

5. P_1: Without the freedom to buy and sell, the freedom to speak is absent.
   P_2: In the absence of a free market, tyranny flourishes.
   C: A free market is necessary for a free society.

6. P_1: He jests at scars that never felt a wound.
   P_2: Mercutio jests at scars.
   C: Mercutio never felt a wound.

7. P_1: It takes years and years for adult Americans to learn to speak the French language well.
   P_2: In France even little children speak the French language well.
   C: The French are the most intelligent people in the world.

8. P_1: If the world has not existed from eternity, then at some time there was nothing at all.
   P_2: Out of nothing at all nothing at all could come.
   C: The world has existed from eternity.

9. P$_1$: The world must have existed from eternity.
    P$_2$: Eternity includes 6006 B.C.
    C: The world must have existed in 6006 B.C.

10. P$_1$: There are many average families in the United States.
    P$_2$: The average U.S. family has 2.2 children.
    P$_3$: Two-tenths of a child is a part of a child.
    C: Many U.S. families have parts of children in them.

1.2

1. This is not an argument but rather an explanation of why the beaker exploded.

2. This is an argument with the conclusion that it is undoubtable that there are flying saucers.

3. This is an argument with the conclusion that John probably ate something that did not agree with him.

4. This is not an argument. Rather it is an explanation of why John stayed home from the dance.

5. This is not an argument but rather a conditional statement.

6. This is not an argument but rather a conditional statement.

7. This is not an argument but rather an illustration.

8. This is an argument with the conclusion that the world is in much greater danger of a nuclear confrontation than one might at first think.

9. This is not an argument but rather a string of statements that amount more of less to a description.

10. This is an argument with the conclusion that a government cannot be considered responsible if it does not deal with the problem of inflation.

1.3

1. Inductive argument: an inductive generalization.

2. Deductive argument.

3. Inductive argument: an argument based on signs.

4. Inductive argument from effect to cause.

5. Inductive argument: an argument from analogy.

6. Inductive argument: a prediction.

7. Deductive argument.

8. Inductive argument: a prediction.

9. Inductive argument: an argument from analogy.

10. Deductive argument.

1.4

1. Weak inductive argument.

2. Valid deductive argument. It is based on the fact that a standard deck of playing cards has 52 cards in it and that 52 minus 1 is 51.

3. Fairly strong inductive argument.

4. Valid deductive argument.

5. Weak inductive argument.

6. Valid deductive argument.

7. Invalid deductive argument.

8. Weak inductive argument. Since there are many colors in the spectrum that are not red and only one color (namely, red itself) that is red, it is not likely that John's favorite color is red.

9. Weak inductive argument.

10. Strong inductive argument.

1.5

1. This argument has the form

> All F are V.
> All V are A.
> Therefore, all F are A.

This is a valid argument form and every substitution instance of it, including the given one, is valid.

2. This argument has the form

> All F are V.
> Some B are F.
> Therefore, some B are V.

This is a valid argument form and every substitution instance of it, including the given one, is valid.

3. This argument has the form

    All *F* are *V*.
    Some *B* are *V*.
    Therefore, some *B* are *F*.

    This is an invalid argument form. It has the following substitution instance in which the premises are true and the conclusion is false:

    All fish are vertebrates.
    Some bears are vertebrates.
    Therefore, some bears are fish.

4. This argument has the form

    No *G* are *B*.
    All *M* are *B*.
    Therefore, no *G* are *M*.

    This is a valid argument form; all substitution instances of it are valid, including the given one.

5. This argument has the form

    No *G* are *B*.
    Some *M* are *B*.
    Therefore, no *M* are *G*.

    This is an invalid argument form. It has the following substitution instance in which the premises are true and the conclusion is false:

    No plants are animals.
    Some living things are animals.
    Therefore, no living things are plants.

6. This argument has the form

    Some *L* are *P*.
    Some *L* are *M*.
    Therefore, some *P* are *M*.

    This is an invalid argument form. It has the following substitution instance in which the premises are true and the conclusion is false:

    Some animals are dogs.
    Some animals are cats.
    Therefore, some dogs are cats.

7. This argument has the form

    Some *M* are *E*.
    All *G* are *M*.
    Therefore, some *E* are *G*.

This is an invalid argument form. It has the following substitution instance in which the premises are true and the conclusion is false:

> Some human beings are females.
> All men are human beings.
> Therefore, some females are men.

8. This argument has the form

> Some L are T.
> No J are L.
> Therefore, some T are not J.

This is a valid argument form and every substitution instance of it, including the given one, is valid.

9. This argument has the form

> All B are D.
> No D are F.
> Therefore, no B are F.

This is a valid argument form, and all substitution instances of it, including the given one, are valid.

10. This argument has the form

> All T are C.
> All T are B.
> Therefore, all C are B.

This is an invalid argument form. It has the following substitution instance in which the premises are true and the conclusion is false:

> All dogs are animals.
> All dogs are mammals.
> Therefore, all animals are mammals.

1.6

1.

2.

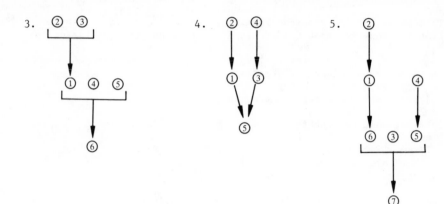

3. 4. 5.

CHAPTER 2

2.1

1. positive; horse
2. negative; horse
3. negative; lawyer
4. negative; doctor
5. negative; woman, older woman
6. negative; alcoholic
7. positive; elderly person
8. negative; athlete
9. positive; minister, priest, rabbi
10. positive; gun

2.2

1. Human being, professional person, doctor, surgeon.

2. Pecan tree, tree, plant, living thing.

3. Peach tree, fruit tree, tree, plant.

4. Physical object, tool, wrench, metric wrench, box-end metric wrench.

5. This is a series of increasing intension and decreasing extension.

6. Triangle: three-sided plane figure.
    Right triangle: three-sided plane figure, containing one right
       angle.
    Isosceles triangle: three-sided plane figure, two sides of equal
       length.
    Equilateral triangle: three-sided plane figure, all three sides
       of equal length.

7. The extension of "ghost" is empty, i.e., the empty class.
    The extension of "number that equals its own square" is the number 1,
       i.e., the class containing only the number 1.

    (Zero is not counted as a number.)

    The extension of "last king of France" is Louis XVIII, i.e., the
       class containing only Louis XVIII.
    The extension of "rational number whose square is 2" is empty,
       i.e., the empty class.
    The extension of "perfect square number between 1 and 100" is
       1, 4, 9, 16, 25, 36, 49, 64, 81, and 100 (i.e., the set
       containing these numbers), provided that "between" is under-
       stood inclusively. If "between" is understood exclusively,
       then 1 and 100 are not included.

8. a. Plane figure, polygon, less than five sides, etc.
    b. Plane figure, polygon, all sides of equal length, etc.
    c. Animal, mammal, four-legged, etc.
    d. Material object, useful object, etc.

9. Whole number between 1.2 and 1.25; king of France in 1980; mother
    of Adam; first man on the moon in 1950; unicorn.

10. First man on the moon; whole number between 1 and 3; President of
    the United States in 1980; father of Isaac; author of *A Concise
    Introduction to Logic*.

2.3

1. Religion is the opiate of the masses.
    Religion is the supreme road to happiness.

2. This is both a stipulative definition (since the word "entropy"
    is first given a meaning by it) and a theoretical definition (since
    it is defined in terms of the theory and has logical implications
    for the theory).

3. This is a stipulative definition. Insofar as it is part of a mathe-
    matical theory, it is also a theoretical definition.

4. This is a persuasive definition (since it is intended to create
    a positive attitude toward death).

5. This is a lexical definition.

1. A square is a rectangle with all sides of equal length.
   A circle is a plane figure in which every point is equidistant
   from some fixed point.
   An even number is a whole number evenly divisible by 2.
   An odd number is a whole number not evenly divisible by 2.

2. This is an operational definition.

3. This is a definition by subclass.

4. This is an ostensive or demonstrative definition.

5. An entity is ductile if and only if, when it is pulled from two
   opposite directions, it stretches without breaking. An entity is
   malleable if and only if, when it is hammered, it flattens without
   cracking.

6. A marsupial is a kangaroo, a possum, and the like.
   An ungulate is a horse, a cow, a goat, and the like.

7. No. Stipulative definitions that are part of a theory and
   determine the contents of that theory are also theoretical definitions.

8. A junior college is a college in which only courses for the first
   two years, the freshman and sophomore years, are offered. This
   is a definition by genus (college) and difference (in which only
   courses for the first two years are offered).

9. Mercury, Venus, Earth, Mars, Jupiter, Saturn, Neptune, Uranus,
   Pluto.

10. This is a synonymous definition.

2.5

1. This definition is too broad.

2. This definition is too narrow in that it fails to include horses
   that are neither ridden nor used to do work. It is also too broad
   in that it includes elephants, oxen, and the like. Additionally,
   the word "large" is vague to some extent.

3. This definition fails to indicate the context (poker) to which the
   definiens belongs.

4. This definition is too narrow in that it fails to include tables
   with three legs, for example. It is too broad in that it
   includes benches and stools.

5. This definition is expressed in metaphorical and vague language.

6. The most prominent defect of this definition is its use of affective (abusive) language. It is also both too broad and too narrow,
   and it contains a metaphor.

7. This definition is expressed in metaphorical and vague language.

8. This definition is too broad: someone may believe something true without having any good reason for doing so. This belief would certainly not count as knowledge.

9. This definition is expressed in vague and obscure language. It may also be circular.

10. This definition of a common object is framed in obscure language. Also, it is too narrow: some balls, e.g., those used as globes or teaching devices, may not have "nonutilitarian functionality."

CHAPTER 3

3.1

1. "Miscarriage" in the first premise means a premature discharge of a fetus. In the conclusion the same word means a *breach* (of justice).

2. The premise means that people buy and eat more of Sloppy Joe's hamburgers than anyone else's hamburgers. But the conclusion "understands" the premise to mean that each one of Sloppy Joe's hamburgers has more already eaten out of it.

3. The premise is true because no matter what is done a wart will sooner or later go away (being a viral infection that the body sooner or later fights off). But this does not lead to the conclusion that killing the toad by the light of the full moon will cure warts.

4. To be a superb thief means to be superb at thieving. But to be a superb man is not to be both a man and a superb thief: it is to be a man with excellent qualities, especially of the moral sort. That is, "superb" is used in different senses.

5. "Heavy-hearted" does not mean with a (literally) heavy heart. It means sad and downcast.

3.2

1. This is either false cause (if the meaning of the claim is that the dream caused the heart attack or if the meaning of the claim is that the future heart attack caused the past dream) or hasty generalization (if the meaning of the claim is that Mary always has such dreams before disasters).

2. Ad populum.

3. False cause.

4. Hasty generalization.

5. This is missing the point: ERA is a matter of equal *rights*, not equal size.

6. Accident.

7. Accident.

8. Ad hominem abusive.

9. Ad hominem circumstantial.

10. Appeal to authority. A military figure is not necessarily a reliable authority about educational or fiscal policy.

11. Missing the point. This is a question of morals, not behavior.

12. Ad ignorantiam.

13. Appeal to pity.

14. Appeal to force.

15. False cause.

16. False cause (post hoc ergo propter hoc).

17. Appeal to ignorance.

18. Missing the point.

19. Tu quoque version of ad hominem.

20. Ad populum. Despite the fact that the appeal is to be different from the crowd, it is still to the person's vanity or at least to the person's self-esteem.

3.3

1. Equivocation (on "arms").

2. Division.

3. Begging the question.

4. Amphiboly.

5. Amphiboly.

6. Complex question.

7. False dichotomy.

8. Amphiboly.

9. Equivocation (on "you'll never eat anyplace else again").

10. Amphiboly.

11. Equivocation (on "glued to his seat").

12. Division.

13. Equivocation (on "had" and on "seasoned").

14. Division.

15. This is difficult to assess but is probably best assessed as equivocation (on "normalcy"). The word "normalcy" does not change meaning in one sense in this example, but in another sense, normalcy for cats and dogs is not the same notion as normalcy for birds or people.

16. Composition.

17. Amphiboly.

18. Division.

19. Equivocation (on "light").

20. Composition.

3.4

1.	Slippery slope.	11.	Slippery slope.
2.	Weak analogy.	12.	Straw man.
3.	Red herring.	13.	Red herring.
4.	Suppressed evidence.	14.	Red herring.
5.	Suppressed evidence.	15.	Suppressed evidence.
6.	Weak analogy.	16.	Straw man.
7.	Suppressed evidence.	17.	Weak analogy.
8.	Slippery slope.	18.	Weak analogy.
9.	Weak analogy.	19.	Weak analogy.
10.	Weak analogy.	20.	Slippery slope.

CHAPTER 4

4.3

1. "All men are mortals." This is true. The corresponding propositions are computed as

   I: true   E: false   O: false

2. "Some fish are not bass." This is true. The corresponding propositions are computed as

   A: false   E: undetermined   I: undetermined

3. "No dogs are cats." This is true. The corresponding propositions are computed as

   A: false   I: false   O: true

4. "Some chairs are antiques." This is true. The corresponding propositions are computed as

    A: undetermined   E: false   O: undetermined

5. "Some grasshoppers are not insects." This is false. The corresponding propositions are computed as

    A: true   I: true   E: false

6. "All numbers are even numbers." This is false. The corresponding propositions are computed as

    E: undetermined   I: undetermined   O: true

7. "No authors are poets." This is false. The corresponding propositions are computed as

    A: undetermined   I: true   O: undetermined

8. "Some horses are palominos." This is true. The corresponding propositions are computed as

    A: undetermined   E: false   O: undetermined

9. "No roses are plants." This is false. The corresponding propositions are computed as

    A: undetermined   I: true   O: undetermined

10. "Some elms are not trees." This is false. The corresponding propositions are computed as

    A: true   E: false   I: true

4.4

1. Some fish are non-bass.
2. All non-principalities are non-angels.
3. All non-butterflies are ants.
4. All perfect things are non-mortals.
5. Some cats are non-dogs.
6. No non-gods are non-idols.
7. No non-wives are workers.
8. All non-insects are non-spiders.
9. Some poets are not authors.
10. Some wolves are females.

4.8

1. All survivors are strong things.

2. No persons who are not in the club are persons who are allowed to vote.

3. All places to which you go are places to which I will follow you.

4. All tigers are fierce things.

5. All men who will be promoted are sergeants.

6. All men who will be promoted are sergeants.

7. All elephants are big animals.

8. All non-miscreants are persons who will go unpunished, and no miscreants are persons who will go unpunished.

9. All persons identical with George Washington are persons who were the first U.S. president.

10. All persons identical with my father are persons who were carpenters.

11. Some men (*or*: some men who are near this place) are men who are at work (*or*: are men who are at this time at work).

12. All whales are mammals.

13. All times in the future are times when I will meet you.

14. No dogs are five-legged things.

15. All men who are well-fed are men who are content.

16. No persons are persons who like broccoli.

17. All persons who like broccoli are persons who love spinach. (This translation assumes that the word "you" in the proposition is used impersonally. If it is used personally, then the translation should be: All persons identical with you who like broccoli are persons who love spinach.)

18. All cities that have industry are prosperous cities.

19. Some people are people who did not like the movie.

20. All times identical to the time when you first called are times when I was surprised.

CHAPTER 5

5.1, I

1. All *P* are *M*.
   Some *S* are *M*.
   Some *S* are *P*.   *invalid*

2. All *M* are *P*.
   All *M* are *S*.
   All *S* are *P*.   *invalid*

3.　No P are M.
　　Some M are S.
　　Some S are not P.　*valid*

4.　Some M are P.
　　No S are M.
　　All S are P.　　*invalid*

5.　Some P are not M.
　　Some S are not M.
　　Some S are not P.　*invalid*

6.　No P are M.
　　All S are M.
　　No S are P.　　*valid*

7.　All P are M.
　　Some M are not S.
　　Some S are P.　　*invalid*

8.　No M are P.
　　No M are S.
　　Some S are not P.　*invalid*

9.　No M are P.
　　Some S are not M.
　　Some S are not P.　*invalid*

10.　No P are M.
　　All M are S.
　　No S are P.　　*invalid*

5.1, II

1.　P = men
　　S = continents
　　M = islands

This argument is of form **EAO-4**. It is invalid. (On the assumption that islands exist, it is valid.)

2.　P = men
　　S = continents
　　M = islands

This argument is of form **EIO-3**. It is valid.

3.　P = seals
　　S = tigers
　　M = walruses

This argument if of form **IEO-4**. It is invalid.

4.　P = large animals
　　S = elephants
　　M = pachyderms

In standard form the argument becomes:

　　Some pachyderms are not large animals.
　　All elephants are pachyderms.
　　Some elephants are not large animals.

This argument is of form **OAO-1**. It is invalid.

5.　P = felines
　　S = dogs
　　M = cats

In standard form the argument becomes:

```
All cats are felines.
No dogs are cats.
No dogs are felines.
```

This argument is of form **AEE**-1. It is invalid.

6. *P* = dogs
    S = spaniels
    M = cockers

This argument is of form **IAO**-4. It is invalid.

7. *P* = stallions
    S = horses
    M = roans

In standard form the argument becomes:

```
All roans are stallions.
Some horses are roans.
Some horses are stallions.
```

This argument is of form **AII**-1. It is valid.

8. *P* = insects
    S = grasshoppers
    M = ants

In standard form the argument becomes:

```
No ants are insects.
All ants are grasshoppers.
No grasshoppers are insects.
```

This argument is of form **EAE**-3. It is invalid.

9. *P* = paintings
    S = art objects
    M = figurines

In standard form the argument becomes:

```
No paintings are figurines.
All figurines are art objects.
Some art objects are not paintings.
```

This argument is of form **EAO**-4. It is invalid. (On the assumption that figurines exist, it is valid.)

10. *P* = racers
    S = drivers
    M = speeders

In standard form the argument becomes:

All racers are speeders.
No speeders are drivers.
No drivers are racers.

This argument is of form **AEE**-4.   It is valid.

1. Invalid

2. Invalid

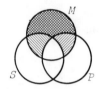

3. Valid

4. Invalid

5. Invalid

6. Valid

7. Invalid

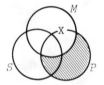

8. Invalid

9. Invalid

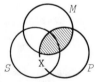

10. Invalid

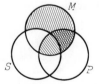

126

1. Invalid (valid existentially)   6. Invalid

2. Valid   7. Valid

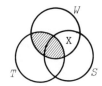

3. Invalid   8. Invalid

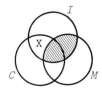

4. Invalid   9. Invalid (valid existentially)

5. Invalid   10. Valid

127

1. All P are M. S is distributed in the conclusion but not in
    All M are S.   the minor premise, so this commits the fallacy
    All S are P.   of illicit minor.

2. All M are P.   This argument is valid.
    All S are M.
    All S are P.

3. No P are M.   This argument commits the fallacy of drawing
    Some S are M.   an affirmative conclusion from a negative
    Some S are P.   premise.

4. No M are P.   Having two negative premises, this argument
    No M are S.   commits the fallacy of exclusive premises.
    No S are P.

5. All M are P.   This argument is valid.
    Some M are S.
    Some S are P.

6. Some P are not M. P is distributed in the conclusion but not in
    All M are S.   the major premise, so this argument commits
    Some S are not P.   the fallacy of illicit major.

7. Some M are P.   This argument commits the fallacy of drawing
    No S are M.   an affirmative conclusion from a negative
    All S are P.   premise.

8. All M are P.   This argument commits the fallacy of drawing an
    No M are S.   affirmative conclusion from a negative premise.
    All S are P.

9. All M are P. P is distributed in the conclusion but not in
    No S are M.   the major premise, so this argument commits the
    No S are P.   fallacy of illicit major.

10. Some M are P.   This argument is valid.
    All M are S.
    Some S are P.

5.4

1. With P = sane persons, S = financiers, and M = persons, this is
    equivalent to **AII**-1. It is valid.

2. With P = valid arguments, S = chains of reasoning, and M = intelli-
    gible arguments, this is equivalent to **AIO**-2. It is invalid.

3. With P = solvent persons, S = happy persons, and M = bankers, this
    is equivalent to **OEO**-3. It is invalid.

4. With P = snacks, S = nutritious foods, and M = fattening foods,
    this is equivalent to **AEE**-4. It is valid.

5. With P = felons, S = scholars, and M = innocent persons, this is equivalent to **EIO**-2. It is valid.

<u>5.5</u>

1. All drinks are things that I like.
   <u>All things identical to this one are drinks.</u>
   All things identical to this one are things that I like.

   This is the syllogism **AAA**-1. It is valid.

2. All times you go to town are times you buy a dress.
   <u>All times identical to today are times you go to town.</u>
   All times identical to today are times you buy a dress.

   This is the syllogism **AAA**-1. It is valid.

3. No immoral acts are fattening acts.
   <u>All acts of overeating are fattening acts.</u>
   No acts of overeating are immoral acts.

   This is the syllogism **EAE**-2. It is valid.

4. All places you will go are places to which I will follow you.
   <u>No places identical with Bali are places to which I will follow you.</u>
   No places identical with Bali are places you will go.

   This is the syllogism **AEE**-2. It is valid.

5. All bits of money you have are bits of money we will spend.
   <u>Some bits of money you have are ill-gotten gains.</u>
   Some ill-gotten gains are bits of money we will spend.

   This is the syllogism **AII**-3. It is valid.

CHAPTER 6

<u>6.1</u>

1. $\sim(A \cdot B)$
2. $\sim A \cdot \sim B$
3. $(\sim A \vee \sim C) \cdot B$
4. $\sim(A \vee B)$
5. $(A \vee B) \supset \sim C$

6. $A \supset (B \cdot \sim C)$
7. $\sim A \equiv (B \cdot C)$
8. $\sim A \supset (\sim B \cdot \sim C)$
9. $A \equiv \sim(B \cdot C)$
10. $A \supset (\sim C \supset B)$

<u>6.2</u>

1. $A \supset (B \supset X)$

   T   T   F

   F

   (F)

2. $\sim A \vee [X \supset (\sim X)]$

   F T   F   T F

   T

   (T)

3. $(A \equiv X) \equiv (B \equiv Y)$

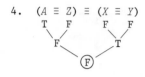

7. $[(A \cdot B) \cdot C] \equiv [A \cdot (X \vee Y)]$

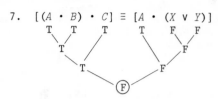

4. $(A \equiv Z) \equiv (X \equiv Y)$

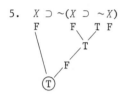

8. $[(\sim A) \equiv (\sim X)] \vee (Y \vee C)$

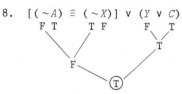

5. $X \supset \sim(X \supset \sim X)$

F   F   T   F

6. $(A \vee X) \supset (Y \vee Z)$

T   F   F   F

9. $[(X \supset Y) \supset \sim Y] \supset \sim X$

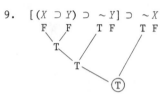

10. $[X \supset (\sim X \supset Y)] \supset [(Y \supset \sim Z) \supset X]$

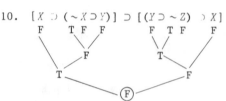

6.3, I   (The truth tables will be omitted in these answers.)

1. Tautology.
2. Contingency.
3. Self-contradiction.
4. Contingency.
5. Contingency.

6. Tautology.
7. Tautology.
8. Self-contradiction.
9. Contingency.
10. Contingency.

6.3, II

1. Not logically equivalent.
2. Logically equivalent.
3. Not logically equivalent.
4. Logically equivalent.
5. Logically equivalent.

6.4

1. *Modus ponens.*
2. *Modus tollens.*
3. Disjunctive syllogism.
4. Hypothetical syllogism.
5. Constructive dilemma.

6. Destructive dilemma.
7. *Modus ponens.*
8. *Modus tollens.*
9. Disjunctive syllogism.
10. Hypothetical syllogism.

<u>6.5</u> (Truth tables omitted.)

1. Valid.	6. Invalid.
2. Valid.	7. Valid.
3. Invalid.	8. Invalid.
4. Valid.	9. Valid.
5. Invalid.	10. Valid.

<u>6.6</u>

1. Valid.

2. Valid.

3. Valid.

4. Valid.

5. Invalid. P false and Q true will make the premises true and the conclusion false.

6. Valid.

7. Valid.

8. Valid.

9. Invalid. P true and Q false will make the premises true and the conclusion false.

10. Invalid. Either P true and Q false or P false and Q true will make the premise true and the conclusion false.

CHAPTER 7

<u>7.1</u>

(1)	4.	$Y \supset Z$	1, 2, MP	(6)	4.	$X \supset Z$	1, 2, HS
	5.	Z	3, 4, MP		5.	$\sim X$	3, 4, MT
(2)	4.	$Y \lor Z$	1, 2, DS	(7)	5.	X	3, 4, DS
	5.	Z	3, 4, DS		6.	$Y \supset Z$	1, 5, MP
					7.	$Z \supset W$	2, 5, MP
(3)	4.	$\sim Y$	1, 2, DS		8.	$Y \supset W$	6, 7, HS
	5.	$\sim Z$	3, 4, MT				
(4)	5.	X	2, 3, MP	(8)	5.	$\sim X$	3, 4, MT
	6.	$Y \lor Z$	1, 5, MP		6.	$Y \cdot Z$	1, 5, DS
	7.	Z	4, 6, DS		7.	W	2, 6, MP
(5)	4.	X	2, 3, DS	(9)	5.	$\sim \sim X$	2, 3, MT
	5.	$\sim Y \supset \sim Z$	1, 4, MP		6.	$\sim Y$	1, 5, DS
	6.	$\sim Z$	2, 5, MP		7.	W	4, 6, DS

131

(10)   5. $X \supset \sim Y$ 1, 3, MP
       6. $\sim Y$ 3, 5, MP
       7. $\sim T$ 2, 6, DS
       8. $\sim W$ 4, 7, MT

7.2

(1)   4. $X \vee Y$ 3, Add
      5. Z 1, 4, MP
      6. $Z \vee T$ 5, Add
      7. W 2, 6, MP

(2)   5. X 3, 4, MP
      6. $Y \cdot Z$ 1, 5, MP
      7. Y 6, Simp
      8. K 2, 7, MP

(3)   5. $Y \vee Z$ 1, 4, MP
      6. $(Y \supset W) \cdot (Z \supset K)$ 2, 3, Conj
      7. $W \vee K$ 5, 6, CD

(4)   4. $\sim Y$ 3, Simp
      5. $\sim X$ 1, 4, MT
      6. $\sim X \vee W$ 5, Add
      7. K 2, 6, MP
      8. $K \vee T$ 7, Add

(5)   4. $\sim X$ 3, Simp
      5. $\sim Y$ 2, Simp
      6. $Y \vee Z$ 1, 4, DS
      7. Z 5, 6, DS
      8. $Z \vee T$ 7, Add

(6)   4. $K \cdot L$ 2, Simp
      5. K 4, Simp
      6. $X \vee Z$ 3, 5, MP
      7. $Y \vee W$ 1, 6, CD

(7)   4. $X \supset Y$ 1, Simp
      5. $Y \supset Z$ 2, Simp
      6. $X \supset Z$ 4, 5, HS
      7. $(X \supset Y) \supset W$ 3, 6, MP
      8. W 4, 7, MP

(8)   5. $\sim L$ 3, Simp
      6. $\sim(X \cdot Y)$ 2, 5, MT
      7. $Z \cdot W$ 1, 6, DS
      8. Z 7, Simp
      9. $N \cdot O$ 4, 8, MP
      10. N 9, Simp

(9)   5. $X \supset Y$ 1, Simp
      6. X 2, Simp
      7. Y 5, 6, MP
      8. M 3, 5, MP
      9. $Y \cdot M$ 7, 8, Conj
      10. $Z \cdot K$ 4, 9, MP
      11. Z 10, Simp
      12. $Z \vee W$ 11, Add

(10) 5. X 2, Simp
      6. P 1, 5, MP
      7. $Q \cdot S$ 3, 6, MP
      8. Q 7, Simp
      9. $P \cdot Q$ 6, 8, Conj
      10. $P \equiv Q$ 4, 9, MP

(11) 4. A 2; Simp
      5. $B \supset C$ 1,4; MP
      6. B 3; Simp
      7. C 5,6; MP
      8. $C \cdot A$ 4,7; Conj

(12) 5. $\sim X$ 3; Simp
      6. $\sim A$ 2,5; MT
      7. $\sim(B \supset C)$ 1,6; MT
      8. $\sim D$ 4,7; MT
      9. $\sim A \cdot \sim D$ 6,8; Conj

(13) 5. $A \supset B$ 1; Simp
      6. $B \supset E$ 2; Simp
      7. $A \supset E$ 5,6; HS
      8. $H \cdot I$ 3,7; MP
      9. H 8; Simp
      10. J 4,9; MP
      11. $H \cdot J$ 9,10; Conj

132

(14) 6. A 4; Simp
      7. B 3,6; MP
      8. $A \cdot B$ 6,7; Conj
      9. $C \lor D$ 1,8; MP
      10. $D \supset G$ 5; Simp
      11. $(C \supset E) \cdot (D \supset G)$ 2,10; Conj
      12. $E \lor G$ 9,10; CD
      13. $(A \cdot B) \cdot (E \lor G)$ 8,12; Conj

(15) 5. $\sim C$ 3,4; MT
      6. A 2,5; DS
      7. B 1,6; MP
      8. $B \cdot \sim C$ 5,7; Conj
      9. $(B \cdot \sim C) \lor E$ 8; Add

7.3

(1)   4. $\sim X \lor \sim Y$ 1, DM
      5. $\sim \sim X$ 2, DN
      6. $\sim Y$ 4, 5, DS
      7. Z 3, 6, DS

(2)   4. $(X \cdot Y) \lor (X \cdot Z)$ 1, Dist
      5. $X \cdot Z$ 2, 4, DS
      6. $Z \cdot X$ 5, Com
      7. K 3, 6, MP

(3)   4. X 3, Simp
      5. $\sim \sim X$ 4, DN
      6. Y 1, 5, DS
      7. $\sim \sim Y$ 6, DN
      8. Z 2, 7, DS
      9. $X \cdot Y$ 4, 6, Conj
      10. $(X \cdot Y) \cdot Z$ 8, 9, Conj

(4)   3. $\sim Z \cdot \sim W$ 2, DM
      4. $\sim Z$ 3, Simp
      5. $\sim(X \lor Y)$ 1, 4, MT
      6. $\sim X \cdot \sim Y$ 5, DM
      7. $\sim Y \cdot \sim X$ 6, Com
      8. $\sim Y$ 7, Simp

(5)   4. X 1, Simp
      5. $(Y \cdot Z) \cdot X$ 1, Com
      6. $Y \cdot Z$ 5, Simp
      7. Y 6, Simp
      8. $Z \cdot Y$ 6, Com
      9. Z 8, Simp
      10. $Y \cdot X$ 4, 7, Conj
      11. $W \cdot T$ 2, 10, MP
      12. W 11, Simp
      13. $Y \cdot W$ 7, 12, Conj
      14. $(Y \cdot W) \cdot Z$ 9, 13, Conj

(6)   4. $\sim T \cdot W$ 2, Com
       5. $\sim T$ 4, Simp
       6. $\sim\sim X$ 1, 5, MT
       7. X 6, DN
       8. $X \lor Y$ 7, Add
       9. Z 3, 8, MP
     10. W 2, Simp
     11. $W \cdot Z$ 9, 10, Conj

(7)   3. $\sim X \lor \sim Y$ 1, Add
       4. $\sim(X \cdot Y)$ 3, DM
       5. $\sim W$ 2, 4, MP
       6. $\sim W \lor \sim Z$ 5, Add
       7. $\sim(W \cdot Z)$

(8)   2. $\sim X \cdot \sim\sim X$ 1, DM
       3. $\sim X$ 2, Simp
       4. $\sim\sim X \cdot \sim X$ 2, Com
       5. $\sim\sim X$ 4, Simp
       6. X 5, DN
       7. $X \lor Y$ 6, Add
       8. Y 3, 7, DS

(9)   4. $X \lor \sim Y$ 1, Add
       5. $\sim Y \lor X$ 4, Com
       6. Z 2, 5, MP
       7. $X \cdot Z$ 1, 6, Conj
       8. $\sim\sim(X \cdot Z)$ 7, DN
       9. W 3, 8, DS
     10. $W \cdot X$ 1, 9, Conj
     11. $(W \cdot X) \cdot Z$ 6, 10, Conj

(10) 3. X 1, Simp
       4. $X \lor Y$ 3, Add
       5. $Y \lor X$ 4, Com
       6. $\sim W$ 2, 5, MP
       7. $\sim Z \cdot X$ 1, Com
       8. $\sim Z$ 7, Simp
       9. $\sim Z \cdot \sim W$ 6, 8, Conj
     10. $\sim(Z \lor W)$ 9, DM

(1) 3. $X \vee \sim Y$ 1, Add
        4. $\sim Y \vee X$ 3, Com
        5. $Y \supset X$ 4, Impl
        6. Z 2, 5, MP
        7. $X \cdot Z$ 1, 6, Conj

(2) 3. $\sim X \vee Y$ 1, Impl
        4. $Y \vee \sim X$ 3, Com
        5. $Y \supset Z$ 2, 4, MP
        6. $X \supset Z$ 1, 5, HS
        7. $\sim Z \supset \sim X$ 6, Trans

(3) 3. $X \cdot Y$ 1, 2, Conj
        4. $(X \cdot Y) \vee (\sim X \cdot \sim Y)$ 3, Add
        5. $X \equiv Y$ 4, Equiv

(4) 3. $X \vee Y$ 1, Add
        4. $Y \vee X$ 3, Com
        5. $\sim \sim Y \vee X$ 4, DN
        6. $\sim Y \supset X$ 5, Impl
        7. $(X \supset \sim Y) \cdot (\sim Y \supset X)$ 2, 6, Conj
        8. $X \equiv \sim Y$

(5) 3. $\sim X \vee Y$ 1, Impl
        4. $\sim X \vee Z$ 2, Impl
        5. $(\sim X \vee Y) \cdot (\sim X \vee Y)$ 3, 4, Conj
        6. $\sim X \vee (Y \cdot Z)$ 5, Dist
        7. $X \supset (Y \cdot Z)$ 6, Impl

(6) 2. $\sim X \vee (Y \cdot Z)$ 1, Impl
        3. $(\sim X \vee Y) \cdot (\sim X \vee Z)$ 2, Dist
        4. $(X \supset Y) \cdot (\sim X \vee Z)$ 3, Impl
        5. $(X \supset Y) \cdot (X \supset Z)$ 4, Impl

(7) 3. $\sim X \vee Z$ 1, Impl
        4. $\sim Y \vee Z$ 2, Impl
        5. $Z \vee \sim X$ 3, Com
        6. $Z \vee \sim Y$ 4, Com
        7. $(Z \vee \sim X) \cdot (Z \vee \sim Y)$ 5,6, Conj
        8. $Z \vee (\sim X \cdot \sim Y)$ 7, Dist
        9. $Z \vee \sim (X \vee Y)$ 8, DM
     10. $\sim (X \vee Y) \vee Z$ 9, Com
     11. $(X \vee Y) \supset Z$ 10, Impl

(8) 2. $\sim (X \vee Y) \vee Z$ 1, Impl
        3. $Z \vee \sim (X \vee Y)$ 2, Com
        4. $Z \vee (\sim X \cdot \sim Y)$ 3, DM
        5. $(Z \vee \sim X) \cdot (Z \vee \sim Y)$ 4, Dist
        6. $(\sim X \vee Z) \cdot (Z \vee \sim Y)$ 5, Com
        7. $(\sim X \vee Z) \cdot (\sim Y \vee Z)$ 6, Com
        8. $(X \supset Z) \cdot (\sim Y \vee Z)$ 7, Impl
        9. $(X \supset Z) \cdot (Y \supset Z)$ 8, Impl

(9)	3.	$\sim X \vee (X \cdot Y)$	1, Impl
	4.	$(\sim X \vee X) \cdot (\sim X \vee Y)$	3, Dist
	5.	$\sim X \vee X$	4, Simp
	6.	$X \vee \sim X$	5, Com
	7.	$[(Y \cdot X) \vee (\sim X \cdot Y)] \supset Y$	2, Com
	8.	$[(Y \cdot X) \vee (Y \cdot \sim X)] \supset Y$	7, Com
	9.	$[Y \cdot (X \vee \sim X)] \supset Y$	8, Dist
	10.	$\sim[Y \cdot (X \vee \sim X)] \vee Y$	9, Impl
	11.	$Y \vee \sim[Y \cdot (X \vee \sim X)]$	10, Com
	12.	$Y \vee [\sim Y \vee \sim(X \vee \sim X)]$	11, DM
	13.	$(Y \vee \sim Y) \vee \sim(X \vee \sim X)$	12, Assoc
	14.	$\sim(X \vee \sim X) \vee (Y \vee \sim Y)$	13, Com
	15.	$(X \vee \sim X) \supset (Y \vee \sim Y)$	14, Impl
	16.	$Y \vee \sim Y$	6, 15, MP
	17.	$\sim Y \vee Y$	16, Com
	18.	$Y \supset Y$	17, Impl

(10)	4.	$\sim(X \cdot Y) \vee X$	1, Impl
	5.	$X \vee \sim(X \cdot Y)$	4, Com
	6.	$X \vee (\sim X \vee \sim Y)$	5, Dist
	7.	$(X \vee \sim X) \vee \sim Y$	6, Assoc
	8.	$\sim Y \vee (X \vee \sim X)$	7, Com
	9.	$\sim \sim Y$	2, DN
	10.	$X \vee \sim X$	8, 9, DS
	11.	$\sim X \vee X$	10, Com
	12.	$X \supset X$	11, Impl
	13.	X	3, 12, MP
	14.	$X \cdot Y$	2, 13, Conj

(11)	3.	$A \supset (\sim \sim B \vee C)$	1; DN
	4.	$A \supset (\sim B \supset C)$	3; Impl
	5.	$(A \cdot \sim B) \supset C$	4; Exp
	6.	$(\sim B \cdot A) \supset C$	5; Comm
	7.	$\sim B \supset (A \supset C)$	6; Exp
	8.	$A \supset C$	2,7; MP

(12)	3.	$\sim A \vee (B \vee C)$	1; Impl
	4.	$\sim A \vee (C \vee B)$	3; Comm
	5.	$(\sim A \vee C) \vee B$	4; Assoc
	6.	$\sim \sim (\sim A \vee C) \vee B$	5; DN
	7.	$\sim (\sim A \vee C) \supset B$	6; Impl
	8.	$\sim (\sim A \vee C) \supset C$	2,7; HS
	9.	$\sim \sim (\sim A \vee C) \vee C$	8; Impl
	10.	$(\sim A \vee C) \vee C$	9; DN
	11.	$\sim A \vee (C \vee C)$	10; Assoc
	12.	$\sim A \vee C$	11; Taut
	13.	$A \supset C$	12; Impl

(13) 2. $(\sim A \lor B) \supset (B \supset A)$ 1; Impl
     3. $(\sim A \lor B) \supset (\sim B \lor A)$ 2; Impl
     4. $\sim (\sim A \lor B) \lor (\sim B \lor A)$ 3; Impl
     5. $(\sim \sim A \cdot \sim B) \lor (\sim B \lor A)$ 4; DeM
     6. $(A \cdot \sim B) \lor (\sim B \lor A)$ 5; DN
     7. $(\sim B \lor A) \lor (A \cdot \sim B)$ 6; Comm
     8. $[(\sim B \lor A) \lor A] \cdot [(\sim B \lor A) \lor \sim B]$ 7; Dist
     9. $(\sim B \lor A) \lor A$ 8; Simp
     10. $\sim B \lor (A \lor A)$ 9; Assoc
     11. $\sim B \lor A$ 10; Taut
     12. $B \supset A$ 11; Impl

(14) 3. $A \cdot \sim B$ 1,2; Conj
     4. $\sim \sim A \cdot \sim B$ 3; DN
     5. $\sim (\sim A \lor B)$ 4; DeM
     6. $\sim (A \supset B)$ 5; Impl
     7. $\sim (A \supset B) \lor \sim (B \supset A)$ 6: Add
     8. $\sim [(A \supset B) \cdot (B \supset A)]$ 7; DeM
     9. $\sim (A \equiv B)$ 8; Equiv

(15) 3. $\sim [(A \supset B) \cdot (B \supset A)]$ 1; Equiv
     4. $\sim (A \supset B) \lor \sim (B \supset A)$ 3; DeM
     5. $A \lor \sim B$ 2; Add
     6. $\sim B \lor A$ 5; Comm
     7. $B \supset A$ 6: Impl
     8. $\sim \sim (B \supset A)$ 7; DN
     9. $\sim (B \supset A) \lor \sim (A \supset B)$ 4; Comm
     10. $\sim (A \supset B)$ 8,9; DS
     11. $\sim (\sim A \lor B)$ 10; Impl
     12. $\sim \sim A \cdot \sim B$ 11; DeM
     13. $\sim B \cdot \sim \sim A$ 12; Comm
     14. $\sim B$ 13; Simp

7.5

(1)   2. Y CP
         3. $Y \lor X$ 2, Add
         4. $X \lor Y$ 3, Com
         5. $Z \cdot W$ 1, 4, MP
         6. $W \cdot Z$ 5, Com
         7. W 6, Simp
     8. $Y \supset W$ 2-7, CP

(2)   2. $X \cdot W$ CP
         3. X 2, Simp
         4. $W \cdot X$ 2, Com
         5. W 4, Simp
         6. $X \lor Y$ 3, Add
         7. $(Z \lor W) \supset R$ 1, 6, MP
         8. $W \lor Z$ 5, Add
         9. $Z \lor W$ 8, Com
         10. R 7, 9, MP
     11. $(X \cdot W) \supset R$ 2-10, CP

137

(3)   3. $X \lor Z$ CP
         4. $(X \supset Y) \cdot (Z \supset W)$ 1, 2, Conj
         5. $Y \lor W$ 3, 4, CD
     6. $(X \lor Z) \supset (Y \lor W)$ 3-5, CP

(4)   3. $X \cdot Z$ CP
         4. X 3, Simp
         5. Y 1, 4, MP
         6. $Z \cdot X$ 3, Com
         7. Z 6, Simp
         8. W 2, 7, MP
         9. $Y \cdot W$ 5, 8, Conj
    10. $(X \cdot Z) \supset (Y \cdot W)$ 3-9, CP

(5)   2. X CP
         3. $X \lor Y$ 2, Add
         4. $(Z \lor W) \supset R$ 1, 3, MP
             5. Z CP
             6. $Z \lor W$ 5, Add
             7. R 4, 6, MP
         8. $Z \supset R$ 5-7, CP
     9. $X \supset (Z \supset R)$ 2-8, CP

(6)   3. $\sim Y \cdot \sim W$ CP
         4. $\sim Y$ 3, Simp
         5. $\sim X$ 1, 4, MT
         6. $\sim W \cdot \sim Y$ 3, Com
         7. $\sim W$ 6, Simp
         8. $\sim Z$ 2, 7, MT
         9. $\sim X \cdot \sim Z$ 5, 8, Conj
    10. $(\sim Y \cdot \sim W) \supset (\sim X \cdot \sim Z)$ 3-9, CP

(7)   3. X CP
         4. $Y \cdot Z$ 1, 3, MP
         5. $Z \cdot Y$ 4, Com
         6. Z 5, Simp
     7. $X \supset Z$ 3-6, CP
         8. Z CP
         9. $X \cdot W$ 2, 8, MP
        10. X 9, Simp
    11. $Z \supset X$ 8-10, CP
    12. $(X \supset Z) \cdot (Z \supset X)$ 7, 11, Conj
    13. $X \equiv Z$ 12, Equiv

(8)   3. X CP
         4. $X \lor Y$ 3, Add
         5. Z 1, 4, MP
     6. $X \supset Z$ 3-5, CP
         7. $\sim X$ CP
         8. $\sim X \lor \sim L$ 7, Add
         9. $\sim Z \cdot \sim W$ 2, 8, MP
        10. $\sim Z$ 9, Simp
    11. $\sim X \supset \sim Z$ 7-10, CP
    12. $Z \supset X$ 11, Trans
    13. $(X \supset Z) \cdot (Z \supset X)$ 6, 12, Conj
    14. $X \equiv Z$ 13, Equiv

(9)   3. $X \lor Z$ CP
      4. $(X \supset Y) \cdot (Z \supset Y)$ 1, 2, Conj
      5. $Y \lor Y$ 3, 4, CD
      6. Y 5, Taut
   7. $(X \lor Z) \supset Y$ 3-6, CP

(10) 3. $\sim X \lor \sim Y$ 1, DM
      4. $\sim Y \lor \sim X$ 3, Com
      5. $\sim Z \lor \sim(Y \lor W)$ 2, DM
      6. $\sim Z \lor (\sim Y \cdot \sim W)$ 5, DM
      7. $(\sim Z \lor \sim Y) \cdot (\sim Z \lor \sim W)$ 6, Dist
      8. $\sim Z \lor \sim Y$ 7, Simp
      9. $\sim Y \lor \sim Z$ 8, Com
      10. Y CP
      11. $\sim\sim Y$ 10, DN
      12. $\sim X$ 4, 11, DS
      13. $\sim Z$ 9, 11, DS
      14. $\sim X \cdot \sim Z$ 12, 13, Conj
   15. $Y \supset (\sim X \cdot \sim Z)$ 10-14, CP

7.6

(1)   2. $\sim(Y \lor \sim Y)$ IP
      3. $\sim Y \cdot \sim\sim Y$ 2, DM
   4. $Y \lor \sim Y$ 2-3, IP

(2)   3. $\sim(Z \lor W)$ IP
      4. $\sim Z \cdot \sim W$ 3, DM
      5. $\sim Z$ 4, Simp
      6. $\sim Y$ 2, 5, MT
      7. $Y \cdot X$ 1, Com
      8. Y 7, Simp
      9. $Y \cdot \sim Y$ 6, 8, Conj
   10. $Z \lor W$ 3-9, IP

(3)   3. $\sim\sim X$ IP
      4. X 3, DN
      5. Y 1, 4, MP
      6. $\sim Y$ 2, 5, MP
      7. $Y \cdot \sim Y$ 5, 6, Conj
   8. $\sim X$ 3-7, IP

(4) 4. $Z \lor \sim Y$ 3, Com
     5. $\sim Z$ IP
     6. $\sim Y$ 4, 5, DS
     7. $\sim X$ 2, 6, MT
     8. X 1, 7, MP
     9. $X \cdot \sim X$ 7, 8, Conj
   10. Z 5-9, IP

(5)   6. $\sim(T \lor U)$ IP
      7. $\sim T \cdot \sim U$ 6, DM
      8. $\sim T$ 7, Simp
      9. $T \lor \sim Y$ 3, Com
      10. $\sim Y$ 8, 10, DS
      11. $\sim X$ 1, 10, MT

139

```
     12.  Z                  5, 11, MP
     13.  W                  2, 12, MP
     14.  ~U • ~T            7, Com
     15.  ~U                 14, Simp
     16.  ~W                 4, 15, MP
     17.  W • ~W             13, 16, Conj
  18.  T v U                 6-17, IP
```

7.7

```
(1)  / P ⊃ [P • (Q v ~Q)]
          1.  P                      CP
              2.  ~(Q v ~Q)          IP
                  3.  ~Q • ~~Q       2, DM
              4.  Q v ~Q             2, 3, IP
          5.  P • (Q v ~Q)           1, 4, Conj
       6.  P ⊃ [P • (Q v ~Q)]        1, 5, CP
```

```
(2)  / P ⊃ [~P ⊃ (P v P)]
          1.  P                      CP
              2.  ~P                 CP
                  3.  P v P          1, Taut
              4.  ~P ⊃ (P v P)       2-3, CP
          5.  P ⊃ [~P ⊃ (P v P)]     1-4, CP
```

```
(3)  / [(P ⊃ Q) ⊃ P] ⊃ P
          1.  (P ⊃ Q) ⊃ P            CP
          2.  ~(P ⊃ Q) v P           1, Impl
          3.  ~(~P v Q) v P          2, Impl
          4.  (~~P • ~Q) v P         3, DM
          5.  (P • ~Q) v P           4, DN
          6.  P v (P • ~Q)           5, Com
          7.  (P v P) • (P v ~Q)     6, Dist
          8.  P v P                  7, Simp
          9.  P                      8, Taut
       10.  [(P ⊃ Q) ⊃ P] ⊃ P        1-9, CP
```

```
(4)  / (P ⊃ Q) v (P • ~Q)
          1.  ~(P ⊃ Q)               CP
          2.  ~(~P v Q)              1, Impl
          3.  ~~P • ~Q               2, DM
          4.  P • ~Q                 3, DN
       5.  ~(P ⊃ Q) ⊃ (P • ~Q)       1-4, CP
       6.  ~~(P ⊃ Q) v (P • ~Q)      5, Impl
       7.  (P ⊃ Q) v (P • ~Q)        6, DN
```

(5)   / $(P \lor Q) \lor [\sim P \cdot (Q \lor \sim Q)]$

1.	$\sim(P \lor Q)$	CP
2.	$\sim P \cdot \sim Q$	1, DM
3.	$\sim P$	2, Simp
4.	$\sim Q \cdot \sim P$	2, Com
5.	$\sim Q$	4, Simp
6.	$\sim Q \lor \sim Q$	5, Taut
7.	$Q \supset \sim Q$	6, Impl
8.	$\sim P \cdot (Q \supset \sim Q)$	3, 7, Conj
9.	$\sim(P \lor Q) \supset [\sim P \cdot (Q \supset \sim Q)]$	1-8, CP
10.	$\sim\sim(P \lor Q) \lor [\sim P \cdot (Q \supset \sim Q)]$	9, Impl
11.	$(P \lor Q) \lor [\sim P \cdot (Q \supset \sim Q)]$	10, DN

CHAPTER 8

8.1

1. $(x)(Sx \supset Rx)$

2. $(x)[(Sx \cdot Rx) \supset Px]$

3. $(x)[(Sx \cdot Px) \supset (Rx \lor Cx)]$

4. This proposition is ambiguous. If it means that of all things only poisonous snakes are rattlers, then it is to be translated as:

    $(x)[Rx \supset (Px \cdot Sx)]$

    But if it means that of snakes only the poisonous ones are rattlers, then it is to be translated as:

    $(x)[Sx \supset (Rx \supset Px)]$

5. $(\exists x)[(Px \cdot Sx) \cdot Rx]$

6. $(x)[(Rx \cdot Px) \supset Sx]$

7. $(x)[Cx \supset (Rx \equiv \sim Px)]$

8. $(\exists x)[Cx \cdot (Px \supset Sx)]$

9. $(\exists x)[(Px \cdot Sx) \cdot Zx]$

10. $(x)[(Px \cdot Sx) \supset (Dx \cdot Cx)]$

8.2

(1)	4.	$Ax \supset Bx$	1, UI
	5.	$Bx \supset Cx$	2, UI
	6.	$Cx \supset Dx$	3, UI
	7.	$Ax \supset Cx$	4, 5, HS
	8.	$Ax \supset Dx$	6, 7, HS
	9.	$\sim Dx \supset \sim Ax$	8, Trans
	10.	$(x)(\sim Dx \supset \sim Ax)$	9, UG

(2) 3. $Ac \cdot Bc$ 1, UI
      4. Ac 3, Simp
      5. $(\exists x)Ax$ 4, EG
      6. $(\exists x)Cx$ 2, 5, MP

(3) 2. $Ac \cdot Bc$ 1, EI
      3. Ac 2, Simp
      4. $(\exists x)Ax$ 3, EG
      5. $Bc \cdot Ac$ 2, Com
      6. Bc 5, Simp
      7. $(\exists x)Bx$ 6, EG
      8. $(\exists x)Ax \cdot (\exists x)Bx$ 4, 7, Conj

(4) 4. $\sim(x)Ax$ 2, 3, MT
      5. $(x)Bx$ 1, 4, DS
      6. Bc 5, UI
      7. $(\exists x)Bx$ 6, EG

(5) 4. $Ac \lor Bc$ 1, EI
      5. $\sim Ac$ 2, UI
      6. Bc 4, 5, DS
      7. $(\exists x)Bx$ 6, EG
      8. $(x)Cx$ 3, 7, MP
      9. Cx 8, UI
    10. $Cx \lor Dx$ 9, Add
    11. $(x)(Cx \lor Dx)$ 10, UG

(6) 3. $\sim Bc$ 2, EI
      4. $(Ac \cdot Bc) \lor Cc$ 1, UI
      5. $\sim Bc \lor \sim Ac$ 3, Add
      6. $\sim(Bc \cdot Ac)$ 5, DM
      7. $\sim(Ac \cdot Bc)$ 6, Com
      8. Cc 4, 7, DS
      9. $(\exists x)Cx$ 8, EG

(7) 5. $Ac \lor Dc$ 2, EI
      6. $Dc \lor Ac$ 5, Com
      7. $\sim Dc$ 3, UI
      8. Ac 6, 7, DS
      9. Bc 4, UI
    10. $Ac \supset (Bc \supset Cc)$ 1, UI
    11. $Bc \supset Cc$ 8, 10, MP
    12. Cc 9, 11, MP
    13. $(\exists x)Cx$ 12, EG

(8) 3. Ay 2, UI
      4. $Ay \supset By$ 1, UI
      5. By 3, 4, MP
      6. $(x)Bx$ 5, UG

(9) 4. $Ac \cdot Bc$ 1, EI
      5. $Bc \cdot Ac$ 4, Com
      6. Bc 5, Simp
      7. $Bc \supset (Dc \cdot Ec)$ 2, UI
      8. $Dc \cdot Ec$ 6, 7, MP
      9. $Ec \cdot Dc$ 8, Com

10.	Ec	9, Simp
11.	$Ec \supset \sim Fc$	3, UI
12.	$\sim Fc$	10, 11, MP
13.	$(\exists x) \sim Fx$	12, EG

(10)
5.	Ac	3, EI
6.	$Ac \supset Bc$	1, UI
7.	Bc	5, 6, MP
8.	$\sim \sim Bc$	7, DN
9.	$\sim Bc \lor Cc$	2, UI
10.	Cc	8, 9, DS
11.	$\sim Cc$	4, UI
12.	$Cc \lor (x)Ax$	10, Add
13.	$(x)Ax$	11, 12, DS

8.4

(1)
3.	$(x)Ax$	CP
4.	Ax	3, UI
5.	$(\exists x)Ax$	4, EG
6.	$(x)Bx$	1, 5, MP
7.	Bx	6, UI
8.	$(\exists x)Bx$	7, EG
9.	$(x)Cx$	2, 8, MP
10.	$(x)Ax \supset (x)Cx$	3-9, CP

(2)
2.	Ax	CP
3.	$Ax \lor Bx$	3, Add
4.	$(Ax \lor Bx) \supset (Cx \cdot Dx)$	1, UI
5.	$Cx \cdot Dx$	3, 4, MP
6.	Cx	5, Simp
7.	$Ax \supset Cx$	2-6, CP
8.	$(x)(Ax \supset Cx)$	7, UG

(3)
2.	Ax	CP
3.	$(\exists x)Ax$	2, EG
4.	$(x)(Bx \cdot Cx)$	1, 3, MP
5.	$Bx \cdot Cx$	4, UI
6.	$Cx \cdot Bx$	5, Com
7.	Cx	6, Simp
8.	$Ax \supset Cx$	2-7, CP
9.	$(x)(Ax \supset Cx)$	8, UG

(4)
3.	Bx	CP
4.	$Bx \lor Ax$	3, Add
5.	$Ax \lor Bx$	4, Com
6.	$(\exists x)(Ax \lor Bx)$	5, EG
7.	$(x)(Cx \cdot Dx)$	1, 6, MP
8.	$Cx \cdot Dx$	7, UI
9.	$Dx \cdot Cx$	8, Com
10.	Dx	9, Simp
11.	$Bx \supset Dx$	3-10, CP
12.	$(x)(Bx \supset Dx)$	11, UG
13.	$(x)Ex$	2, 12, MP
14.	Ex	13, UI
15.	$(\exists x)Ex$	14, EG

143

(5)   4. Ex CP
        5. $\sim\sim Ex$ 4, DN
        6. $\sim\sim Ex \lor \sim Dx$ 5, Add
        7. $\sim Dx \lor \sim\sim Ex$ 6, Com
        8. $\sim(Dx \cdot \sim Ex)$ 7, DM
        9. $Bx \supset (Dx \cdot \sim Ex)$ 2, UI
       10. $\sim Bx$ 8, 9, MT
       11. $\sim Bx \lor \sim Cx$ 10, Add
       12. $\sim(Bx \cdot Cx)$ 11, DM
       13. $(Bx \cdot Cx) \lor Ax$ 1, UI
       14. Ax 12, 13, DS
       15. $Ax \supset Fx$ 3, UI
       16. Fx 14, 15, MP
   17. $Ex \supset Fx$ 4-16, CP
   18. $(x)(Ex \supset Fx)$ 17, UG

8.5

(1) Let universe be a, b. Let Aa = T, Ba = T, Ab = T (or F), Bb = F.
Argument becomes

    1. $(Aa \cdot Ba) \lor (Ab \cdot Bb)$ / $Ba \cdot Bb$

Its truth table shows the premise true and the conclusion false:

$(Aa \cdot Ba) \lor (Ab \cdot Bb)$ // $Ba \cdot Bb$
    T T T [T] T F F   T [F] F

(2) Let universe be a, b. Let Aa = T, Ba = T, Ca = T, Ab = F, Bb = F,
Cb = T (or F). Argument becomes

    1. $(Aa \supset Ba) \cdot (Ab \supset Bb)$
    2. $(Aa \cdot Ca) \lor (Ab \cdot Cb)$ / $Ba \cdot Bb$

Its truth table shows the premises true and the conclusion false:

$(Aa \supset Ba) \cdot (Ab \supset Bb)$ / $(Aa \cdot Ca) \lor (Ab \cdot Cb)$ // $Ba \cdot Bb$
    T T T [T] F T F   T T T [T] F F T   T [F] F

(3) Let universe be a. Let Aa = F, Ba = T (or F), Ca = T (or F),
Da = T. Argument becomes

    1. $Aa \supset (Ba \cdot Ca)$
    2. $Ca \supset Da$ / $Da \supset Aa$

Its truth table shows the premises true and the conclusion false:

$Aa \supset (Ba \cdot Ca)$ / $Ca \supset Da$ // $Da \supset Aa$
    F [T] T T T   T [T] T   T [F] F

(4) Let universe be a, b. Let Aa = F, Ba = T (or F), Ab = T, Bb = F.
Argument becomes

    1. $(Aa \cdot Ab) \supset (Ba \cdot Bb)$ / $(Aa \supset Ba) \cdot (Ab \supset Bb)$

144

Its truth table shows the premise true and the conclusion false:

$(Aa \cdot Ab) \supset (Ba \cdot Bb)$ // $(Aa \supset Ba) \cdot (Ab \supset Bb)$
F   F   T $\boxed{\text{T}}$ T   F   F   F   T   T $\boxed{\text{F}}$ T   F   F

(5) Let universe be a. Let Aa = F, Ba = T. Argument becomes

     1. $Aa \supset Ba$ / $Aa \equiv Ba$

Its truth table shows the premise true and the conclusion false:

$Aa \supset Ba$ // $Aa \equiv Ba$
F $\boxed{\text{T}}$ T   F $\boxed{\text{F}}$ T

8.6, I

1. $(x)(Px \supset {\sim}Txj)$

2. $(x)(Px \supset {\sim}Txx)$

3. $(x)[Px \supset (\exists y)(Py \cdot Lxy)]$

4. $(x)[Px \supset {\sim}(y)(Py \supset Lxy)]$

5. $(x)[Px \supset {\sim}(y)(Py \supset Lyx)]$

6. $(x)\{Px \supset (\exists y)[(Py \cdot Tyx) \cdot Lxy]\}$

7. $(\exists x)\{Px \cdot (y)[(Py \cdot Tyx) \supset Lxy]\}$

8. $(x)\{Px \supset (y)[(Py \cdot {\sim}Tyx) \supset {\sim}Lxy]\}$

9. $(x)\{Px \supset (\exists y)[(Py \cdot Tyx) \cdot {\sim}Lxy]\}$

10. $(x)\{Px \supset (y)[(Py \cdot {\sim}Tyx) \supset Lxy]\} \supset (x)(Px \supset Lxx)$

8.6, II

(1)   3. $(x)Fxc$ 2, EI
       4. Fxc 3, UI
       5. $(\exists y)Fxy$ 4, EG
       6. $(x)(\exists y)Fxy$ 5, UG
       7. $(x)Gxx$ 1, 6, MP

(2)   2. $(y)Fxy$ 1, UI
       3. Fxx 2, UI
       4. $(\exists z)Fzz$ 3, EG

(3)   2. $(y)(Fxy \cdot Gyx)$ 1, UI
       3. $Fxx \cdot Gxx$ 2, UI
       4. $(z)(Fzz \cdot Gzz)$ 3, UG

(4) 2. $(\exists x)Fx$ CP
     3. Fc 2, EI
     4. $Fc \supset (y)Gy$ 1, UI
     5. $(y)Gy$ 3, 4, MP
     6. Gc 5, UI
     7. $(\exists y)Gy$ 6, EG
  8. $(\exists x)Fx \supset (\exists y)Gy$ 2-7, CP

(5) 2. $(x)Fx$ 1, Simp
     3. $(y)Gy \cdot (x)Fx$ 1, Com
     4. $(y)Gy$ 3, Simp
     5. Fx 2, UI
     6. Gy 4, UI
     7. $Fx \cdot Gy$ 5, 6, Conj
     8. $(y)(Fx \cdot Gy)$ 7, UG
     9. $(x)(y)(Fx \cdot Gy)$ 8, UG

(6) 3. $(\exists y)Ixy$ 1, UI
     4. Ixa 3, EI
     5. $(y)(Ixy \supset {\sim}Mxy)$ 2, UI
     6. $Ixa \supset {\sim}Mxa$ 5, UI
     7. ${\sim}Mxa$ 4, 6, MP
     8. $(\exists y){\sim}Mxy$ 7, EG
     9. $(x)(\exists y){\sim}Mxy$ 8, UG

(7) In this example, the letters u, v, and w are used as variables, not as constants. In the text the convention is that they are constants. Deviation from the conventions of the text is employed here to make the proof easier to follow and to avoid complexities in instantiating.

    3. $Buvw$ CP
    4. $(y)(z)[Buyz \supset (Luy \cdot Lyz)]$ 1, UI
    5. $(z)[Buvz \supset (Luv \cdot Lvz)]$ 4, UI
    6. $Buvw \supset (Luv \cdot Lvw)$ 5, UI
    7. $Luv \cdot Lvw$ 3, 6, MP
    8. Luv 7, Simp
    9. $Lvw \cdot Luv$ 7, Com
   10. Lvw 9, Simp
   11. $(y)(Luy \supset {\sim}Iuy)$ 2, UI
   12. $Luv \supset {\sim}Iuv$ 11, UI
   13. ${\sim}Iuv$ 8, 12, MP
   14. $(y)(Lvy \supset {\sim}Ivy)$ 2, UI
   15. $Lvw \supset {\sim}Ivw$ 14, UI
   16. ${\sim}Ivw$ 10, 15, MP
   17. ${\sim}Iuv \cdot {\sim}Ivw$ 13, 16, Conj
   18. ${\sim}(Iuv \vee Ivw)$ 17, DM
  19. $Buvw \supset {\sim}(Iuv \vee Ivw)$ 3-18, CP
  20. $(z)[Buvz \supset {\sim}(Iuv \vee Ivz)]$ 19, UG
  21. $(y)(z)[Buyz \supset {\sim}(Iuy \vee Iyz)]$ 20, UG
  22. $(x)(y)(z)[Bxyz \supset {\sim}(Ixy \vee Iyz)]$ 21, UG

(8) 4. $(y)(z)[Bxyz \supset (Lxy \cdot Lyz)]$ 1, UI
    5. $(z)[Bxxz \supset (Lxx \cdot Lxz)]$ 4, UI
    6. $Bxxz \supset (Lxx \cdot Lxz)$ 5, UI
     7. $Bxxz$ IP
     8. $Lxx \cdot Lxz$ 6, 7, MP

9.	Lxx	8, Simp
10.	Ixx	2, UI
11.	$(y)(Ixy \supset \sim Lxy)$	3, UI
12.	$Ixx \supset \sim Lxx$	11, UI
13.	$\sim Lxx$	10, 12, MP
14.	$Lxx \cdot \sim Lxx$	9, 13, Conj
15.	$\sim Bxxz$	7–14, IP
16.	$(y) \sim Bxxy$	15, UG
17.	$(x)(y) \sim Bxxy$	16, UG

(9)

3.	$\sim Ixy$	CP
4.	$(y)[(Lxy \cdot Lyx) \supset Ixy]$	2, UI
5.	$(Lxy \cdot Lyx) \supset Ixy$	4, UI
6.	$\sim (Lxy \cdot Lyx)$	3, 5, MT
7.	$\sim Lxy \lor \sim Lyx$	6, DM
8.	$Lxy \supset \sim Lyx$	7, Impl
9.	$\sim Lyx$	CP
10.	$(y)(Lxy \lor Lyx)$	1, UI
11.	$Lxy \lor Lyx$	10, UI
12.	$Lyx \lor Lxy$	11, Com
13.	Lxy	9, 12, DS
14.	$\sim Lyx \supset Lxy$	9–13, CP
15.	$(Lxy \supset \sim Lyx) \cdot (\sim Lyx \supset Lxy)$	8, 14, Conj
16.	$Lxy \equiv \sim Lyx$	15, Equiv
17.	$\sim Ixy \supset (Lxy \equiv \sim Lyx)$	3–16, CP
18.	$(y)[\sim Ixy \supset (Lxy \equiv \sim Lyx)]$	17, UG
19.	$(x)(y)[\sim Ixy \supset (Lxy \equiv \sim Lyx)]$	18, UG

(10)

3.	$(\exists y)Lxy$	CP
4.	Lxa	3, EI
5.	$(y)(Lxy \supset Lyx)$	2, UI
6.	$Lxa \supset Lax$	5, UI
7.	Lax	4, 6, MP
8.	$Lxa \cdot Lax$	4, 7, Conj
9.	$(y)(z)[(Lxy \cdot Lyz) \supset Lxz]$	1, UI
10.	$(z)[(Lxa \cdot Laz) \supset Lxz]$	9, UI
11.	$(Lxa \cdot Lax) \supset Lxx$	10, UI
12.	Lxx	8–11, MP
13.	$(\exists y)Lxy \supset Lxx$	3–12, CP
14.	$(x)[(\exists y)Lxy \supset Lxx]$	13, UG

CHAPTER 9

9.1

1. Direct method of agreement.
2. Inverse method of agreement.
3. Method of difference.
4. Method of concomitant variation.
5. Double method of agreement.

9.2

1. $1 - 1/13 = 12/13$
2. $1/52$
3. $(13 + 4 - 1)/52 = 16/52 = 4/13$
4. $(1/52)/(1/4) = 4/52 = 1/13$
5. $[(52 - 16)/52]/[(52 - 13)/52] = 36/39 = 12/13$
6. $12/52 = 3/13$
7. $6/36 = 1/6$
8. $2/36 = 1/18$
9. $2/6 = 1/3$
10. $3/5$

9.3

1. Unclear base for the percentage.

2. Sample, being all ministers, is biased. It does not fairly represent the general population.

3. Dispersion is ignored.

4. Characteristic attributed is not independent of the desires and purposes of those doing the attributing.

5. The meaning of average is not specified. Only if the *mode* is 19.6 years would this be a valid argument. Otherwise, some measure of the mean and the dispersion would be required to justify this conclusion.